THE CURE

FOR THE CHRONIC LIFE

DEANNA FAVRE & SHANE STANFORD

THE CURE
FOR THE CHRONIC LIFE

OVERCOMING

THE HOPELESSNESS

THAT HOLDS YOU BACK

Abingdon Press
Nashville

THE CURE FOR THE CHRONIC LIFE: OVERCOMING THE HOPELESSNESS THAT HOLDS YOU BACK

This book is printed on acid-free paper.

Library of Congress Cataloging-in-Publication Data

Favre, Deanna.
  The cure for the chronic life : overcoming the hopelessness that holds you back / Deanna Favre & Shane Stanford.
    p. cm.
  ISBN 978-1-4267-1001-8 (book - hardback/adhesive casebound, with dust jacket : alk. paper)
    1. Christian life. 2. Worry—Religious aspects—Christianity. 3. Hope--Religious aspects—Christianity. I. Stanford, Shane, 1970- II. Title.
  BV4501.3.F38 2010
  248.4--dc22

                          2010027888

Scripture quotations, unless noted otherwise, are taken from the *Holy Bible*, New Living Translation, copyright © 1996. Used by permission of Tyndale House Publishers, Inc., Wheaton, Illinois 60189. All rights reserved.

Where noted, scripture quotations are taken from *The Message*. Copyright © by Eugene H. Peterson 1993, 1994, 1995, 1996, 2000, 2001, 2002. Used by permission of NavPress Publishing Group.

Scripture quotations noted NIV are taken from the Holy Bible, NEW INTERNATIONAL VERSION®. Copyright © 1973, 1978, 1984 by International Bible Society. All rights reserved throughout the world. Used by permission of International Bible Society.

10 11 12 13 14 15 16 17 18 19—10 9 8 7 6 5 4 3 2 1

MANUFACTURED IN THE UNITED STATES OF AMERICA

FROM DEANNA—

For my family—
Brett, Brittany, Breleigh, and Parker—
I love you.

FROM SHANE—

For Pokey and my girls—
Sarai Grace, Juli Anna, and Emma Leigh—
You are my CURE.

CONTENTS

FOREWORD

We get stuck. Stuck in routines, pain, patterns, and stages. Stuck in swamps of regrets, obligations, and rejections. Stuck in the quicksand of debt, drugs, and fear. We get stuck.

And we pay a price for our stuckness: stale marriages, dependence on mood-altering drugs, addiction to games, holidays, and pastimes. Neglect of our relationships, our souls and, most of all, our God.

Getting unstuck? It's possible. Not easy or quick, but certainly possible. In this book, Deanna and Shane toss out a rope and give us a tug. They have filled these pages with stories, suggestions, and practical instruction. I encourage you to grab hold and let them pull. Consider their instruction and practice their forty days of prayer. Who knows, you may be a few weeks away from a fresh start.

MAX LUCADO

Pastor and *New York Times* Bestselling Author

ACKNOWLEDGMENTS

Of all the words we have written, these are some of the most difficult. How do you say thank you to everyone who contributes to a project like this? It seems so daunting, and you are sure you will not think to list all those who mean so much. And so, we say thank you to everyone who has, in one way or another, made this book possible. You are a treasure and a blessing.

However, there are those whose contributions to this project jump off the page.

First, we want to thank our agent, Chip, for his continued support and encouragement. Thanks for believing that our words are worth the hard work of finding a vehicle for them to be read and heard.

For the great folks at Abingdon Press, thanks for believing the CURE can work for others.

For Jana and Pamela, who became our champions in telling the story.

For Pastor Max Lucado. Your foreword was perfect and much appreciated. Thanks for taking time from your busy schedule to assist our project.

For friends and colleagues at the Favre 4 Hope Foundation and at Gulf Breeze United Methodist Church. Thank you for your continued support and for the great work you do to offer a CURE to all those you meet.

For extended family, friends, priests, and pastors, who pray for us and who make the CURE count for so many.

And for our immediate families, who are the best reasons we know to make each day count. This book, but also so much more, is dedicated to you. We love you.

From one writing partner to another in this project, and for how one idea made this more than just another passing comment between two friends. We can't wait to see what God will do.

And for Jesus; what can we say about your blessing and encouragement? Who could ask for anything more, though we know we will—thank you.

HEALING

He has sent me to comfort the brokenhearted.

Isaiah 61:1

A cheerful heart is good medicine, but a broken spirit saps a person's strength.

Proverbs 17:22

"Lord," he said, "if you want to, you can make me well again." Jesus reached out and touched the man. "I want to," he said. "Be healed!"

Luke 5:12-13

What could an HIV-positive minister and the wife of one of the NFL's greatest players have in common? More than one might imagine. Each of us has lived through difficult life situations and illnesses, overcoming the propensity for chronic hopelessness, to discover the transforming grace and strength of God—no matter how much the questions of life seemed unanswerable.

Our friendship was born from one of life's "coincidences." We discovered our common roots as survivors of chronic illness, but also as survivors of those chronic life situations that, oftentimes, come to define our perspectives of self, others, and God. After all, haven't we all asked questions of God when hope seems lost or at least out of grasp?

In this book, we share our personal journeys and offer a word of hope for those going through life's everyday struggles, and we ask the question, "Are you living in crisis or in Christ?" The answer to this question, more than any question we know, determines so much of how we both see the world and our issues. But more important, it also determines how we view the potential of our solutions in Christ.

This book is framed in the language of questions and answers, hope and despair, ache and healing. These are words and phrases that every person will understand, whether from personal experience or from conversations and interactions with others. Regardless, we have all had unanswered questions that seemed to foster unreasonable decisions; feelings of despair that promoted a sense of apathy or discouragement; or the emotional, physical, or spiritual ache that kept us from seeing God in our midst and from living faithfully as God's person in our paths.

These questions, and this journey, affect all of life's situations. And most of the time, we use such language when we feel as though too much is unanswerable, undoable, or unreachable. How many stories or life situations can we recount that point to our uncertainties of a life with far too many questions?

But what about the other side of that language? What about a God who provides answers for our questions, possibilities for our uncertainties, and a new story for the unrecognizable avenues of grace and hope in each of our lives? This book answers *those* questions and provides a picture of hope in spite of our aches and pains—emotionally, relationally, physically, or spiritually. And if that wasn't enough, God's wonderful gift to us through Christ not only addresses these old hurts, habits, and hang-ups, but it also gives us a new path and a new opportunity for grace and healing. More than anything, God's gift and promise to us in Christ is the reason we wrote the book—that God's redeeming love will meet the deepest of our questions and help us begin again. Wouldn't you like to start over?

In fact, the unanswered life can be as simple as a spiritual ache or as complicated as a debilitating disease. It may be as simple as a bad attitude or as complex as a broken or betrayed relationship. Either way, the effects often become habitual and infectious in how we make life decisions and, especially, how we connect with others. This book describes how disconnection, disaffection, and misdirection from life's choices ultimately create more damage than any physical illness could.

The "unanswered life" of broken relationships or misguided intentions, of habitual patterns of poor decisions, or of the wrong answers from the start invariably disrupts our relationships with God and with one another, because, as the effects grow, our natural tendency is to turn "inward" (the original dilemma from the garden of Eden) and to focus more and more on our own self-interests. Relationships become difficult for us, and we struggle to connect to God in the ways he would have us grow in and serve him. But, more intricately, we also struggle to become *who* God has so lovingly and extravagantly prescribed in us, and this is the real shame of the chronic life.

We believe the answers to these questions remain found within our relationship with God, especially as they are shared, expressed, and lived out in faithfulness with each other. But it took a while to learn this. We didn't wake up one day with a supernatural "directional sign" hanging over our heads. No, we lived through the same broken, misguided, often hopeless circumstances that you may be dealing with and that continue to cause your soul to ache. But we discovered that God has a "new normal" for our lives. Throughout Scripture, God provides one example after another of not only *why* the chronic life is not what God intended, but also *how* to restore the potential of such a life once it breaks down.

In searching Scripture for answers about confronting the chronic life of choices, patterns, and problems, we discovered four primary categories for setting a new direction in life: **compassion, understanding, response,** and **encouragement.** These concepts may seem familiar and even simple. But each of these four categories provides a different way to view the world, to disconnect from our self-destructive patterns, and to take up God's purpose for our lives. And these principles also show how living in Christ changes every aspect—yes, we mean *every* aspect—of our lives forever. God's intention for us is that we will be permanently affected and changed. Remember, this is not supposed to be a series of treatable maladies; God expects a CURE.

You may be thinking, how convenient it is that the first letters of each of the four categories of answers form the word *CURE.* No, it is not a coincidence. Actually, we tweaked the concepts a bit to help you remember these qualities in your life and to enable you to apply them in your journey. But these categories are more than just a play on words or an acronym; they are a connection to how Christ intended for us to live in our world, free from our aches and with our deepest, most important questions answered. Thus, we believe readers will recognize this conversation, as we all confront these broken places from time to time. However, we also believe the impact of the chronic life can complicate other aspects of life. This is not a static issue; with the chronic life, a cascade effect takes place until every part of our life is touched. The results of this pattern for life leave us living "Chronic in Crisis," thus evoking other worries of what the crisis will mean for us. And the cycle continues on from there. But God's plan is different. God wants us to live "Chronic in Christ," throwing off our worries and experiencing the *wonders* of God's love.

This book is framed around a forty-day spiritual treatment plan and devotional guide that provide practical daily connections to life lessons, Scripture, and prayer suggestions. *Forty* is an important number for several reasons. Most important, it represents the number of years the children of Israel wandered in the wilderness and the number of days Jesus spent being tempted by the devil. But the end of any such period in Scripture also marks a major transition point. After forty years, the children of Israel entered into the promised land. And after forty days, Jesus left the wilderness and began his public ministry, which would change the world forever. Most Christians know these stories, but few realize the significance of this period of time for framing and forming the faith that we proclaim and believe today. *Forty* is a period of reflection, renewal, reframing, and restoration that ultimately leads to a **new beginning. How about you? Could you use a "new beginning"?**

God still wants a new and whole life for us today. He no more intends for us to live in an unanswered state or with a chronic pattern of loss and brokenness any more than he intends for us to live in relationship, separate from him. God has a new normal. He has something better, something sweeter in store.

The Cure for the Chronic Life is more than another self-help book. Sure, it provides lessons for living more freely and more faithfully. But it also involves *story*—the stories of our lives; the stories of those whom we love and who have made a difference in our lives; and most important, the story of God and God's love for us. Oh, and by the way, it includes *your* story too. Because the more you read and work through the forty-day spiritual treatment plan day by day, the more you will discover that we are all knitted into this fabric of life together. The lessons of this book work because they are framed by the story of very real problems that plague real people, *every day*. But in the course of your reading and reflection, you will also discover real hope born of God's *very* real love for you and me. And that is the greatest lesson of all.

RECOMMENDED RESOURCES

Favre, Deanna. *Don't Bet Against Me.* Wheaton, Ill.: Tyndale House Publishers, 2008.

Stanford, Shane. *A Positive Life.* Grand Rapids, Mich.: Zondervan, 2010.

CHAPTER ONE

THE SEVEN WORRIES OF LIVING IN CRISIS

Too much of our world understands crisis firsthand. Recent earthquakes in places like Haiti and Chile remind us of the fragile nature of life. In fact, there are "earthquakes" happening every hour of every day for families and individuals through the consequences of poor marriages, abusive childhoods, poor decision patterns—you name it. The debris is strewn from one end of the journey to the other. And when we are dealing with life on these terms, we find ourselves living in the trenches of warfare or in the ruts of complacency. Either way, we are unable to become what God has placed so deeply inside each of us.

But we must survive and so, in response, we learn to live chronically in crisis. And these patterns give birth to worries that permeate every corner of our lives. Soon, we become less about becoming all that God has in store, and instead we spend most of our time enduring what the world has thrown our way. Unfortunately, this sort of life is the most difficult and painful to continue and confront. On the one hand, it is not terminal. It is not the end. Life doesn't transition itself. But on the other hand, it isn't real life either. When we are living in chronic crisis, we are never quite breathing in the fullness of life, but instead holding our breaths, afraid of what might come around the corner. It is chronic, never-ending, all-consuming, but not fatal. Instead, we get the displeasure of living through our illness, for it is powerful enough to drain us of our hope, but not powerful enough to kill us—at least not all at once.

Too often, or as human nature is expected to do, we focus on these worries of life and remain hostage to the whims of this world. And all the while, our souls are craving something more, something different. We crave awe and wonder. We are built for such, to run and to praise—not to be tied down by the meaningless goals and broken relationships.

Most chronic patterns do not start overnight. We do not wake up one morning with a brand-new chronic illness. No, the symptoms develop over time and become debilitating. The result is a life lived at 50 percent power or possibility.

We have a friend who has fought a chronic illness for nearly twenty-five years. We watched this vibrant person in her late thirties teach kindergarten, volunteer at her church, and take care of her family as well as several others. One day her right arm began to ache, until finally, two years later, she found herself in a wheelchair unable to move her legs or arms without significant assistance. The doctors told our friend that she was lucky: the virus had attacked only her limbs and not her torso, thus her major organs were OK. But she would be in a wheelchair the rest of her life. Our friend said she felt "like half of a person—and not the useful half at that." Now, that is not to say that people who use wheelchairs are less than whole persons.

We have lots of friends who live very active, amazing lives in wheelchairs and with other non-traditional circumstances. No, the issue for our friend is that *she* felt like "half of a person" because of what her illness did to her each day. She had imagined that her life would be so different than the circumstances she faced now. In fact, she once said that "living in a wheelchair is not the issue; it is living with the ache that I wish I could get rid of."

Our friend, like millions of other people who deal with long-term and short-term bouts of chronic illness, has made the most of her situation. She is a hero to both of us. But having to face each day with a debilitating chronic illness is not the life we wanted for her. It is not the life her husband or children or family members wanted for her. It is not the life her art teacher and her guitar instructor wanted for her. And it is not the life she wanted either. As she likes to say, she has been "left in the middle of a hurricane and asked to carry on life as normal."

But nothing will be normal again for our friend. So, what has she done? She has learned how to live in her chronically ill body, to maneuver with the help of a wheelchair, and to rely on the love, care, and support of great family and friends. But she has also come to grips with the reality that she will never shoot a basketball again. She cannot hug her sons or cradle a baby. There is so much she *does* because she refuses to live out of fear and loss, but there is so much she *does not do* because her body doesn't respond.

The same is true for our chronic spiritual lives as well. One piece of our "spiritual aircraft" falls off at a time, until the fuselage is in serious trouble. We may still be in the air, but our potential for flight has become seriously limited. We are weighted by the consequences of this life and by the worries that do not give up their place. We must pluck them from our consciousness, our relationships, and our attitudes and move forward to become whole again, and to become what God has in store.

God is offering a new start, a new opportunity to begin again. He is not satisfied with us just getting by. What you have been experiencing in living the chronic life is just not normal to him.

SHANE: At the start of his book *The Purpose Driven Life*, Rick Warren says that "It is not about (us)." I agree totally. But I believe the message is even more substantial. If it "is not about us," that means it can be about someone else: God. And this reality sends an even more important message as we hit the ground and drive the trenches. As we meander through the world thinking that we have it under control, we learn, usually in the most fragile of moments, that not only is it *not about us,* but we also learn that *we are not enough* for the task or journey on which we have embarked. This is a frightening, staggering realization. The story or point of its not being *about us* is sad; this realization of our ineffectiveness and lack of sufficiency while the bullets are flying, while the world caves and the piece shatters in our hands, is downright petrifying.

So, as the apostle Paul would say, "What shall we say about such things?" Sure, the answer is, "If God is for us, who can ever be against us?" (Romans 8:31). But God expects our participation on this one, too. We must confront the worries that have mildewed their way into our lives and leave us partially connected but always suspicious; rationally agreeable but always wary. These worries bloom from the ditches and cover the path rather quickly in our lives. By the time we look up, we can't see the stones that mark the path any longer, and we feel that we are wandering aimlessly in a field. Friend, listen to us . . . under that "field" is the path. We just have to claim it, clean it off, and start walking in the right direction again.

Scripture discusses the broken spirit of a chronic life in **seven worries** that develop from chronically living in crisis. In each of these seven worries, one can see both the expression of a consistently chronic nature that precipitates our way into these patterns and the difficulty in finally relinquishing them. And these seven worries also speak to a unique blunder or brokenness in our souls that is practical and feels all too real. For instance, we can say that one of our worries develops from the accumulation of mental, emotional, and relational garbage, but it is when we begin to name the garbage, putting faces to what has cultivated the pain and bitterness, that things get very real, very fast. And it is not easy. These worries are consuming and devastating for us. Think of it as though we are swimmers weighted with stones that are not large enough to sink us to the bottom, but heavy enough to keep our heads constantly below the surface.

Quite simply, we remember that *we are not enough*. But we also can't let these worries linger, and we can't let them continue pushing the point of our inadequacy back to us. That kind of life is death—death for our hopes, dreams, and relationships. Don't misunderstand us; this life is not easy to confront. But once we do, the process will seem more real and natural than anything we have experienced. Remember, we have been built to crave life. We were born to praise, born to live close to God. And so we must fight to strip away the worries one at a time, no matter how difficult the task may appear or feel.

God wants these seven worries gone, removed from our scope. Period. He wants to take them from us and to offer us something better. Jesus called it "the better way." Peter called it "hope." Paul called it "faith." Regardless, God calls it ours, and he begs us to let go and receive this gift.

So, what about these worries? Let's take a look at "The Seven Worries of Living in Crisis" and what grows from such a path.

WORRY NUMBER ONE:
MEANINGLESS RELATIONSHIPS

SHANE: In my ministry, I have met several young men and women who, over the course of their lives, have reduced themselves or allowed themselves to be reduced to objects or possessions. When I was in seminary, I belonged to a ministry that responded to the needs of prostitutes in our city (both men and women) by assisting with things like food and services for health screenings. I must admit, though, that at first I was reluctant. Having grown up in an ordered, Southern Baptist family, I was raised to believe that good Christian people didn't associate with such folks.

But the more my ministry crossed their lives, the more I discovered these were exactly the kind of people with whom God had called us to associate. Not because we were good and they were bad, or because we could "save them" with our message and service, but because the path of their lives was much like ours, it just looked different to the world. Their sickness and sadness were really no different than those of the alcoholic housewife in my congregation who would rather medicate herself with martinis than face the doubts and decisions of the day or the father of four who used extramarital relationships as a way of masking his deep-seated insecurities.

These prostitutes sold their bodies because they couldn't find anyone to love them for free. The housewife and the father of four sold their souls for the same reason, just in a different market.

One of the prostitutes to whom my wife and I ministered over the years once told us, when we picked her up from jail, that she hated her life but she didn't know how to get out of it. We shared with her about how she could live better, healthier, and wiser. But what struck us most was when she mentioned what she really missed most about life. She said she had lots of "acquaintances" in her business, but very few meaningful relationships. With all that she had been through, the sex, the countless clients, the life of such degradation and despair, what she missed most was having a real friend who cared about her—not her body or what she could do for them, but *her*.

The human experience requires healthy relationships. And in the absence of healthy ones, we will develop and cultivate unhealthy ones. It is that simple. It is how we are wired. What our prostitute friend was saying is that the real broken place in her was the part that connected to people through friendships, not fees. The more mistakes she made, the more she shut off the real part of her life from other people. She had to do that in order to survive, she thought. But it also proved detrimental to real relationships in her life. The chronic life she led kept her from reaching out to others, until all she had was a set of meaningless encounters that said one thing on the surface and absolutely nothing on the inside.

She was created for relationships—beautiful, whole, meaningful relationships. But when life turns in on us, sometimes we will grab hold of whatever relationship we can and then hope that this one might mean something.

One of the worries of the chronic life is a series of meaningless relationships. This is not normal. God has something better in store.

WORRY NUMBER TWO:

THE ACCUMULATION OF MENTAL, RELATIONAL, AND EMOTIONAL GARBAGE

SHANE: Not far from where my family used to live was a large landfill. The community had dealt with this section of town for years. Not only was it unsuitable for building, many considered the chemicals and waste harmful to the health of those who lived in the area, especially the children at the housing project nearby. Eventually the city responded and discovered that the years of accumulation of garbage, rubbish, and other thrown-away materials not only had made the grounds unstable but also had seriously impacted the environment. The community was forced to dig up the garbage, clean out the landfill, and re-soil the area with lime in order to kill any harmful toxins. But even after the land had been "cleaned and restored," still, no one would purchase the property or agree to build. The point is that garbage has as much a mental impact on our community as a physical one.

I have watched friends who have spent years accumulating mental, emotional, and relational garbage in the corners of their lives. They never intended for their lives to be so full of dangerous toxins and effects. But at the end of the day, they are full of rotten, unsafe materials, promises, relationships, patterns, and attitudes that have made their lives almost unbearable.

What can be done? The only option is to clean out the garbage and "re-soil" the landscape so that it can grow healthy again. The problem is that, as with the property in the community where we used to live, a stigma erupts from those around who question whether this life, this area, can be made whole or useable one more time. Many question whether anyone with that kind of garbage can find real redemption after so much baggage. It is a complex dilemma. And to think, it is simply the result of garbage gathering unchecked in our lives. But the repercussions are not simple, and they have long-ranging effects.

The effect of so much garbage is a life filled with almost paralyzing hopelessness. We may not claim it or say it out loud, but at this point, we feel it. It is a life marred with waste, filth, and the prospect or feeling that nothing can be done to clean up the mess. Or at least, that is what the Adversary wants us to believe; quite simply, if he can so manipulate our internal conversations, we remain captive to our illness, living in the garbage.

But God changes that.

I have a friend who lived with garbage piling up for most of his marriage. He made a series of choices that one day led to his wife of twenty-four years walking out the door and taking their teenage children with her. It was a tragic day, and this family will never be the same again. But this was not a surprise to him. You could smell the garbage in his life from miles away. He knew that one day his wife just would not be able to take it any longer. But as so often happens, "one day" came sooner than he had believed.

For each of us, rectifying the chronic life is about, first, cleaning the garbage from the corners of our existence. It is not easy, and it is certainly not a wanted job. After all, who likes to roam through garbage? But even one piece carries the bacteria of an old life, old wound, or old, broken views and attitudes. It all must be gone. That worry cannot be allowed to remain.

And thus, that's worry number two in the chronic life—the accumulation of mental, emotional, and relational garbage. Again, this is not normal. God has something better in store.

WORRY NUMBER THREE:
MISGUIDED PRIORITIES

Unfortunately, as with so many unhealthy patterns, one trouble lands on another making the scene almost unbearable. With a load of meaningless relationships and stacks of mounting garbage, our lives surrender to misguided priorities. At first, we still see the edges of right and wrong. But over time, it is easier to settle with order than to stand up for change or a new direction.

SHANE: I once met a young attorney from a neighboring town who showed up at my office literally looking as though he was about to die. He was pale and nervous. He was sweating profusely, and at first I thought he was having a heart attack. He might as well have been. The truth he shared with me was even more serious.

While representing a young woman who had been arrested both for drug use and for prostitution, this attorney had begun an inappropriate relationship with the woman. Unbeknownst to him, the woman was part of a scheme against the young lawyer, and she had taped their encounters on several occasions. When she revealed the tapes to the young lawyer and divulged the identities of the men who had set her up in the scheme, he knew that he was being targeted for his work on another case, a case in which these other men had a direct connection. They had found an easy prey.

The young lawyer had for many years been headed down a difficult and dangerous path. He and his wife had done well for themselves, and he had made more money in the last five years than he had thought possible. But he also made enemies—people who had long memories and also the means to take advantage of his transgressions. Their answer was a sting operation that would, one way or another, silence the young attorney forever.

I prayed with the young lawyer, who had family friends who had been attending our church for only a short time. His family attended a large church in their own town and were prominent members of the community.

He didn't feel as though he could go to his own pastor, and so, after confiding in one of his friends, the friend suggested that he visit me. We had a long and sad conversation. He knew that his life was about to change and that he had little recourse other than to face the circumstances. But for some reason, as I looked into his eyes, I feared he would choose another road.

Tragically, several days after our visit, the young lawyer's body was found in a dense forest just outside of town. He had taken his own life. In the note that he had left, he talked about the shame he had brought to his family and the pain he would bring to his wife. (His wife had found out about his affair earlier that day, through a letter and videotape.) The young lawyer, whose priorities had spiraled so far out of control, saw only one way out. This worry, in the end, would win.

Friends, God says the worries are not supposed to win, though for so many of us in so many situations, they do.

That is the nature of this worry in the chronic life—a list of misguided priorities that are not easily reframed. But this is not normal. God has something better in store.

WORRY NUMBER FOUR:
THE CREATION OF IDOLS/MAN-MADE GODS

There is a wonderful scene about the power of Creation in the book and movie *Angels and Demons*. [SPOILER ALERT: If you don't want to know what happens in the movie, you may want to skip ahead two paragraphs.] In this scene, the protagonist, Robert Langdon, confronts the "God particle." It is a scientific experiment that "re-creates" the conditions at the very beginning of existence. Of course, as the action ensues to control the power of this experiment, everyone realizes that some things, no matter how much knowledge we have or how much we think we understand, are beyond our grasp. The climax of the scene is when the *camerlengo*, the assistant to the pope, is discovered as the mastermind behind a plot that murdered one pope and threatens the ability of the cardinals to select a second. His fear, as we later discover, is that science will outpace our understanding of God and, worse, replace our need for God.

At the very end of the book and the movie, Robert Langdon is confronted by the newly selected pontiff, whom he saved through the course of events. During their conversation, the pope reminds Robert that God and science do not have to be mutually exclusive. Langdon is not so sure. He sees religion as an impediment to knowledge. The Vatican sees Langdon as a critic bent on tearing down years of tradition. Now, you must realize that this book makes for great fiction, and having great respect for the Catholic Church, we certainly don't believe that there are vast conspiracies and deception behind the walls of the Vatican. But the lessons in the book are about what happens when people build idols to their ways of thinking— mostly without even realizing it. The result is what they thought was incredible scientific advancement was also capable of great destruction, and the church realizes that it no longer lives in a world where it can ignore such conversations.

However, this process is not new. Whether our experiments or situations have been about something as extraordinary as the creation of anti-matter or something as simple as obsessing over having just a little more money to make us feel safe, the chronic life lives the patterns of idol worship well. *How?* you may ask. *Idol worship? But I have never made an idol. I have no golden calves in my home.* Or do you?

We scoff at the children of Israel for creating golden idols when Moses did not respond to their needs in time. We see the idea of idolatry as being confined to ages gone by, when people literally built altars to unseen gods. But idolatry is very much alive and well. The altars have changed and the golden calves are not so shiny, but the impact is still alarming.

Our idols come in the form of dollar bills or bank accounts. Maybe it is a house or a new car. Or possibly it is the new job title. Regardless, the idol is just as powerful because, no matter what it is, its job is to replace God.

Replace God? We would never do that. But wouldn't we? *Don't we?* In fact, we do it every time we allow the world to dictate our worship or our prayer life. We do it every time we allow our circumstances to define how we treat our brothers and sisters. We do it every time we give up or give in instead of holding tighter to God's plan. We most certainly replace God, and the sting is still very real.

In the chronic life, this worry is meant to refocus us. The Adversary doesn't need to destroy us, he simply needs to distract us, only for a moment. That is enough time to reshuffle the deck and change the course. When we look up again, we may not even have realized things have changed.

This worry creates new gods and idols in place of the One who loves us most. But—you guessed it—this is not normal. God has something better in store.

WORRY NUMBER FIVE:
THE TRAP BETWEEN LONELINESS AND SELF-SUFFICIENCY

Once we take the focus off of the important things in life, once the chronic life has taken hold, it doesn't take long to realize that the promises of this world don't ring true. The effects take over and are very real.

Our friend who lives with the chronic illness (the one whom we mentioned earlier) vacillates between bouts of great depression and great self-awareness and self-sufficiency. Both ends of the spectrum are troubling.

The depression signals a degree of loneliness that permeates her soul. You can see it on her wherever she is. At times it debilitates her; at other times it runs her life in quiet ways, not peering above the surface, but you are always sure it is there. When she feels like this, she is fragile (even more so than usual) and insecure. Life seems to control her or, at the very least, she is held hostage by the day.

But the other side of the coin is just as dangerous. During these times, she sparks her strength and moves into the world with a fierceness that is strong and certain. But she is not well enough for the battle; she puts up a good fight but ultimately realizes she has taken on an enemy that is much stronger than she is. During these times, our friend will empty herself, usually for nothing much in particular, until she runs out of steam and is left drained physically and emotionally.

Thinking about the chronic life, we all live this pattern, especially if we bow down to the false gods of our own strength and knowledge every morning. *We are not enough*; sure, we have been over that. But that doesn't seem to matter on those mornings when the day looks either too dark to get out of bed or too easy not to jump over the skyscraper. The truth is that we are still somewhere in the middle, but our heads and our hearts don't know it. And so we jump, either back down into the well or into the bright sky, unaware in either case where we will really land.

By this point, the chronic life has us in its grips. The great pendulum that swings between our weakness and our strength is under its own gravity, and we doubt as to whether we can stop it. We can't—not by ourselves, anyway, and it will continue to swing and make a mockery of our lives until we either beg or jump off this ride.

The trap between loneliness and our false sense of self-sufficiency makes life neither easy nor really worth living. Absolutely, this is not normal. God has something more in store.

WORRY NUMBER SIX:
PARTICIPATING IN UNCONTROLLABLE ADDICTIONS

SHANE: My grandmother used to say that there are some things you just don't talk about, like Uncle Ed's drinking or Aunt Martha's gambling. I never really understood why we couldn't talk about it; after all, everyone—and I mean *everyone*—knew about both.

When I would ask my grandmother why it was such a secret, she always replied, "Some things, sweetheart, are just better kept quiet."

I've thought about this answer for many years. My grandmother was exactly right. After a while, I've learned that some things are just better left in the dark, unsaid and very quiet. Not because they will get better that way. On the contrary, only the light will make them well. But what do you do with a secret or a broken heart or an addiction that is too much for you to deal with or even admit? Most people who are addicted to drugs or alcohol live extremely functional lives. And yet, they are always on the edge. Life has pushed them there, and they teeter between the next hit and the next plunge.

The chronic life is very much like this. We remain in these patterns long enough, and they almost take on the air of addictive behavior—a habit too much to handle or break. It is not that we want to live there either; we don't like what the aches and cravings do to us. But we are petrified at the thought of withdrawal or the uncertainty of taking a new road, the path of which is the only way to be clean again.

And so, we spiral further into our sickness by remaining in a cycle that is too big for us. And we don't speak of it. No one does.

DEANNA: I have met so many people who live in the middle of life. They haven't imploded as yet, but they also haven't reached their potential. And a lot of these people have great resources and fabulous lives—on the surface. But behind the scenes, they are controlled by something more negative.

I know of what I speak here. As I mentioned in my book *Don't Bet Against Me*, my life's journey did not always go as I had planned. Brett and I ran into our share of obstacles in the beginning and spent a great deal of time working our way through one difficult moment after another. For example, it was not easy for me being a single mom, but I also worried about the future and, with so much uncertainty in our lives, the possibility of entering into a marriage covenant that might have no chance of working. We didn't understand the full scope of what such a decision might mean, and so we trudged through the path doing the best we could.

And added to this relational question were the questions we would face years later with Brett's addiction to prescription painkillers and alcohol. For anyone who faces addiction, these questions are profound, frightening, and uncertain. One day, everything is wonderful. The next, the sky is falling. We couldn't move in any real direction, and so we became prisoners to our circumstances. We definitely found ourselves in the midst of a chronic pattern of living.

Yet thankfully, after much prayer, a lot of tough love, and an unbelievable will, Brett kicked both the painkillers and the alcohol. He is, today, the man I first fell in love with and the best father and husband one could imagine. But his journey—our journey—reminds me that all of us are susceptible to the broken places of our souls, and none of us chooses to walk into a shattered life. Over time the broken pieces accumulate, and we wonder if we can get them back in place again. When the chronic nature takes over, we retreat to whatever makes us feel better about ourselves.

The Brett I know today is not the same person as the man of so many years ago. He is the real deal—sweet, determined, caring, genuine. His love for life and his love for his family mean more to him than anything, even football.

But when the chronic life takes over, this worry of uncontrollable decisions and addictions makes us into someone else and then causes us, most tragically, to forget our first loves. As things hit a low point in our lives, I walked out the door of our home and told him that I would not be back until he got himself straight. Brett considers that moment like watching a car wreck in slow motion. His life was whittling away.

That is the Adversary's purpose for the chronic patterns we find ourselves in. Remember, he doesn't have to do it all at once. In fact, I have found Satan to be quite lazy and slothful. He can pick away one piece at a time, until one day, as with a loved one with an addiction problem, we just don't recognize that person anymore.

Worry number six, the worry of participating in uncontrollable addictions, is about becoming "hostage to life." Certainly, this is not normal. God has something more in store.

WORRY NUMBER SEVEN:

TAKING ON BROKEN APPROACHES TO COMMUNITY

SHANE: "I just don't feel like I have any real friends," said the woman sitting across from me in my study.

"Why do you think that is?" was my question.

"I don't know," she said. "But it has made life so difficult, so hard."

We are created to be in relationship. From the beginning of Genesis, the Creator intended for Creation to be intertwined, needing one another just as the image of the Father, Son, and Holy Spirit need one another. That is the "image of God" talked about in Scripture and the critical connection that all of us have to God and to one another.

The chronic life disconnects us from God and from one another. With the other six worries at play, it is easy to see how people find themselves in a pattern where relationships are either hard to come by or difficult to sustain or both.

The real nature of the gospel is that we will find community among those who have believed and followed. That is why Scripture is so intent on reminding us that we have all fallen short of what we were intended to be. We have all missed the boat, so to speak.

But missing the boat in our spiritual walk is just part of the pain the chronic life inflicts. The other side is that we also experience a void of real community and meaningful relationships that then hinder our ability to build and participate in valid, productive interactions.

Does that mean we are anti-social? It can, but not always. Some people are very good at hiding their broken nature and thus never really connecting to anyone.

No, the real result is a series of relationships that are either unhealthy or unreasonable in terms of their objectives or expectations. That is why so many marriages and friendships fail when the chronic life is running rampant. No one will ever be enough to fill the void inside of us. No one. But that does not keep us from saddling our spouses, our children, our parents, and our best friends with those expectations, playing directly into the hands of the Adversary, who by this time has us exactly where he needs us.

The definition of a chronic life is one who consistently participates in a series of actions, deeds, or impressions that become a pattern for defining the self and the relationships in which we participate. Living in these worries, drowned by these self-focused issues and expectations, crumbling under the pressure of addictions, habits, hurts, hang-ups, and self-made gods, we are unable to become what God needs us to be—what we were intended to be from the beginning. In the eyes of heaven, it is a travesty of cosmic proportions.

This worry of the chronic life, like all of the others, is about disruption of our God-given rights, our *imago deo*, our place in the family of God as one of his beloved children. And no matter how many times the world tries to convince us otherwise, no matter how many times it steps into the middle of our lives and causes trouble, no matter how many lies it tells and how many times we believe them, the chronic life is not normal. God has something better in store. God has the CURE.

RECOMMENDED RESOURCE

Manning, Brennan. *The Ragamuffin Gospel.* Sisters, Ore.: Multnomah Publishers, 2005.

THE CURE

For every season, there is a beginning and an ending. Beginnings are easy. Endings? Not so much. It is the same for any part of life and for almost any endeavor we attempt. Football has seasons. Church has seasons. Relationships have seasons. Life has seasons.

The issue is not whether life will change. No, the real issue is whether those of us affected will adjust, assume, and assimilate the change well enough to move forward, understanding that not all change is easy for us, but that all change, in one form or another, is, certainly, about us.

It is about our fears for tomorrow; our dreams for today; our faith in God; and our faith in one another. Change is the crossroads where all of these emotions, certainty, and uncertainty come together. It is where the process is no longer allowed to be mere conjecture, but rather it forces us to live either in its wake or from the bow, charging ahead into the unknown horizons. The difference, as we have discussed, is palpable, personal, and powerful.

What follows in the course of the next several chapters is a spiritual treatment plan for the chronic life. For those of us who have found ourselves in the grips of unhealthy, chronic patterns, this plan will provide you with the opportunity for rest, reflection, and also response as you begin to recover your life from whatever has defined or dominated you. No matter who you are or what you have done, this plan is for you.

And it is also for those of us who have watched the story of a family member or some other loved one unfold and collapse before our very eyes. Hopefully this plan will provide, first, a sense of strength and purpose, reminding us that we are not alone in this process. But it should also give us a presence of mind to view the chronic life no longer as acceptable or unmanageable, either for ourselves or for our loved ones. As we have learned, living chronic in crisis is not normal; God has something better in store for us.

And finally, this spiritual treatment plan is for those of us who have read the worries and see ourselves in each word and phrase, but remain paralyzed by doubt over whether anything can really be done to change our circumstances; or by doubt over the destruction that has already been caused through dishonesty, pain, grief, loss, or uncertainty. If nothing else (but, oh, there is so much more), the CURE becomes our conversation to work out where your next steps lie and whom you need to go along with you on the journey.

Regardless, these sections of the book pull at the tension between the *worries* of this world (which we have already discussed) and the *wonders* that God has in store for us. And, for instance, it is no coincidence that the length of the treatment plan is forty days. *Forty* symbolizes so many things in the Christian faith tradition. Forty days is the length of time the Israelites wandered in the wilderness. Forty is also the number of days Jesus spent preparing his heart and being tempted by the Adversary. Forty represents periods of reconstruction, reflection, repentance, and restoration for

God's journey in each of us. Remember, if you have been living chronic in crisis, again and again, what you have experienced is not normal. We keep repeating the same message because *God has something better in mind*. To grasp this, we must believe it. And that is the struggle. Because the nature of our patterns is chronic, it takes many times, many tries, many attempts to facilitate and believe that a difference can happen. So we repeat this promise over and over again because we *need* to, not just because we want to. Hearing it one more time might make a difference

But if we are to shake the bonds of the chronic life, with its anxieties, doubts, fears, and fragile places, it will happen only as we confront the other side of the story. Hope is found in "alive" places, not the dead ones. And so, the dead places are important only for marking where we do not want to go again. There is only so much we can discover by dwelling in the pain or in the confusion. The answers come when we turn the problems over and look at the other side of the situation. We discover that God has mapped out a path for us different from what the "chronic" impressions of life would have us believe.

Next we must deepen our understanding of what God's Word is telling us and look at life from that new angle of possibilities and opportunities. This forty-day spiritual treatment plan will help you do just that. Certainly, you may not like everywhere this plan will push you or how it will challenge you as you go through it, but it will not leave you in your current place or continuing in those patterns that bring so much grief to your life.

Finally, this plan will give you the opportunity to *deploy* the wonders of God's love through your personal experience, the renewing of your mind, the focus of your heart, and the daily walk of your life. The goal is not only that God's transforming wonders of grace and love deploy themselves into you, but that you then put yourself *into the world*; into the lives of hurting friends and loved ones; into the muddled, confused situations of brokenness; and into the dysfunctional patterns of poor decisions, thus providing a "better way" through your example of God's extravagant, life-changing love.

After all, that is what Jesus required of us, that we would watch and listen for the "better way." In the Bible, when Martha grew frustrated that her sister, Mary, was sitting at Jesus' feet and not helping her serve the guests, Jesus said that Mary had found a "better way."

When Zacchaeus couldn't see Jesus because of the crowds, he climbed a tree and found a "better way."

When the crowd was hungry and growing restless, Jesus took a few fish and some loaves of bread and provided a "better way."

When the woman was going to be publicly put to death for her sins (as the law had given the people in the crowd the right to do), Jesus suggested a "better way" to resolve the matter.

Each of these stories is about a chronic life that reaches a crescendo of confusion before Jesus steps in to unveil the "wonder" of God's love and of God's "better way." For some of these people, it was a matter of having their eyes opened gently; for others it was a matter of life and death if they could not see. Regardless, Jesus met all of them in the worries of their crisis and gave them something that the world could not take away.

The Cure for the Chronic Life invites you to experience Jesus and his healing through Scripture, reflection, prayer, and serving. Each day you work through the forty-day spiritual treatment plan, you will discover what God is saying to you through the words of other servants, some of whom are from Scripture and some of whom are from everyday life. You will then go deeper, taking the focus of God's narrative and implanting it into your own story, as you ask the question, "How does God intend for this to work in me?" Finally, you will deploy what you discover into action through your hands and feet, into the lives of those you meet, or into the lives of those you have met, but who have been waiting to see what happens.

As with all treatment plans, after we have completed the process, we will no longer be the same as when we began—or at least, we shouldn't be the same. God's Word is too profound for that. Our problems are too personal. But also as with other treatment plans, it is important to see the course through and to make it a priority, to follow what the plan serves to teach us and also the random beauty of what God's Spirit plans to show us.

We want very much for you to walk away from these forty days renewed and challenged. We want the presuppositions of your life to be shaken, but the foundation of Christ in you to be more solid than ever. And we want you to experience joy—maybe not in the struggles or pushback that any journey such as this will cause, but in realizing that you never have walked and you never will walk this path alone.

The four parts of the CURE are taken from Scripture and may at first appear to be unusually simple principles to address all of the worries that we previously have discussed. But we believe these principles are so forthright and workable because God understood that our conditions don't require much to hold us back. And so, on the contrary, it doesn't take much to right the ship either. But as we learn, God expects us to get out of our own way and to re-engage with the world. Remember, the chronic life, if nothing else, is about disconnection—from God and from each other. These four simple principles of the CURE will strip us of our seemingly self-sufficient ways and move us back into the places where God works completely and wholly in each of us.

Here is a brief overview of the four principles of the CURE:

1. **Compassion.** *Compassion* literally means to "go beyond one's own struggles to recognize the struggles of others." We can't throw off the chronic life until we have moved out of our own way and are prepared to see the other side of the story through someone else's perspective.

2. **Understanding.** The apostle Paul says that we *transform our spiritual walk with God beginning with the transforming (some say the "renewing") of our minds.* The chronic life limits us in our thinking; in our impressions of the world; in how we see ourselves, God, and others. We can't engage our hearts until we have thrown off the transforming agent the world uses to perpetuate the lie.

3. **Response.** Jesus said, "Your love for one another will prove to the world that you are my disciples" (John 13:35). The chronic life focuses inward to such a degree that we forget the one most important principle—*response*—that Jesus touts throughout the New Testament. Love is the binding factor of faith and of this new life. God is love, the Scripture says, but response is also the means by which people see God's love through us.

4. **Encouragement.** Encouragement means becoming the blessing that we have received in Christ. The chronic life is the opposite, with the focus on *us*. A life of love and encouragement makes the point about *you and me and us together*. There is no more division, no more breakdown focused solely on what we perceive through our dimmed glasses. With encouragement, we see the world as God sees it—one life, one heart, one possibility at a time.

Again, these are simple, forthright principles taken from Scripture. But don't underestimate what God is saying through them. They may appear familiar, but God has much more to say, even through our most recognized concepts, than we can ever assimilate. And better yet, remember, God uses common, ordinary ideas, people, and elements to constantly do the uncommon, extraordinary acts of grace, forgiveness, and restoration.

Before we get started, though, with the four principles of the CURE in mind, here are some helpful tips for your journey over the next forty days.

1. Set aside time that is for you and God. Make your daily time with God a priority, and consider it to be like breathing; without it, you can't survive.

2. Find a translation or a paraphrase of the Bible you like. It might be time to invest in a new Bible. It is worth it; you deserve it. The devotions in this book are based on scriptures taken from *The Message*, which was developed and translated by Eugene Peterson. Thus, you might find it helpful to use that translation. In any regard, choose a Bible translation you connect with most personally.

3. Keep a journal of what you discover, of what God is saying to you and how your life unfolds in the process.

4. Select an accountability partner to make this journey with you. This person doesn't have to be someone who is following the forty-day spiritual treatment plan with you, but perhaps just someone who will ask you—and keep asking—"Have you spent time with God today?"

5. Give yourself a break. Soak in the unfathomable love of God. Be present with him. Nothing more really is needed. God will provide the rest.

6. Know that we have prayed for you—even without knowing what your particular circumstances are—and that you will be blessed by this process. Know also that as God shows up, you will too.

7. Finally, the moments with God in this forty-day spiritual treatment plan follow the outline of the CURE. It is important to work through them in order, as one will lead to another in the process. Be patient. We promise you will see the mark of when you stop living in crisis and start living in Christ. We are already happy and excited for you!

And more than anything, know that we have been rooting for you. We have been where you are and, from time to time, even slip back into old patterns that are just as chronic. But as we have said so many times, living the chronic life is not normal. If you are living the chronic life, what you are experiencing, no matter how much a part of you it has become or how "normal" it feels, is not God's way for you. God has something better in store for you, a better way. Reach out for it. Take hold of it. Treasure it. It is yours. And so is he.

RECOMMENDED RESOURCE

Jones, Laurie Beth. *The Path.* New York: Hyperion, 1998.

CHAPTER THREE

THE CURE: COMPASSION

SHANE: In 1986, I tested positive for HIV. I was born a hemophiliac, and the medicines used to treat my hemophilia were made of human blood. Unfortunately, like treatments for so many hemophiliacs of my generation, my medicines were contaminated. And, so, at sixteen years old, I went to bed one night as the president of my class, the captain of the golf team, and dating the prettiest girl in school. The next day I was told that I had less than three years to live. After adjusting to this life-changing information, I realized—the hard way, mind you—the full nature of how God works in the world. I also learned what the Adversary can do to distract us. I was and am blessed. I had a wonderful family who kept my head on straight. And God always sent the right people and situations to give me care, hope, or love when I needed it the most.

Still, though, for many years, I felt as though the world revolved around me and my story. Some would say that it would be hard for a person *not* to feel this way, given the meds, the doctors, the need to remain focused on your health, and more important, the requirements for fighting the disease and staying healthy.

I thought that living my life, fighting along the journey, and then sharing my testimony with countless groups of people were sufficient for what God needed from me and in me. Years into the journey, I learned that I was wrong. Very wrong.

I did not realize it, but I had slipped into a chronic pattern of life that kept me from the *next* level of God's grace and will. Sure, I had made the "right" life decisions. I had built good, enduring relationships. I even had kept my faith and had the privilege of leading countless others into relationship with Jesus.

But what I was missing in the process of living the good, Christian life was truly being impacted by the life of Christ in the world. As I like to say, it is not enough to love Jesus . . . we must learn to love *like* Jesus, too. I loved Jesus. Everyone could tell that. But I made the focus really only about me and Jesus, thinking that what I dealt with on a daily basis was enough for my witness and serving, and that there was no room for anything else.

Again, I was settling for a comfortable Christian experience. But at a session of the Saddleback Church Global AIDS summit, I sat down next to a woman from southern Africa. Her name was Gutti. (Gutti's birth name was longer and difficult for some people to pronounce, so she preferred this shorter, easier-to-say name.) Gutti was remarkable. She spoke near-perfect English, and when she talked with you, she seemed to light up. She was at the summit as a representative of an orphans' ministry for which she volunteered in South Africa. The ministry sent her to participate in the summit's workshops and to learn from those of us who were the supposed "experts." But it was Gutti who did the teaching. Gutti's story and witness changed my life.

Gutti had been a nurse in one of the larger towns in South Africa and had, from an early age, many advantages not afforded to other women in her village. This included her six sisters, who remained in the local village and who had saved their meager earnings to send their younger sister to the academy to be trained as a nurse. They had chosen Gutti to "make it." The sisters did not have much of a life for themselves, but through their baby sister they could see someone in their family succeed.

Gutti left the village, received her training as a nurse, and proceeded to spend the next seven years working in the hospitals of Johannesburg and other areas. One day she received a message from home that one of her sisters was dying. Gutti returned home just before her oldest sister died from complications due to AIDS. This sister's husband, as many men in the village did, had gone into the city, gotten involved with a prostitute, and not told his wife. His wife died of pneumonia a year after her husband succumbed to the effects of AIDS himself. They left behind four children.

Gutti decided to take the four children and raise them herself, a selfless act in itself. But that was not the end of Gutti's story. After testing many within the village, Gutti learned that her other five sisters were also infected with the AIDS virus. Their husbands also had been with infected partners and had not told their spouses. This is not uncommon in Gutti's village, but during her absence she had forgotten how badly women in general were treated in their society.

Over the next five years, all of Gutti's remaining sisters died of the disease, leaving behind sixteen more children. Altogether, Gutti became the guardian to twenty nieces and nephews. At first, Gutti wondered if she could take care of all the children, But, of course, she also would not allow them to be homeless. She felt almost hopeless when, as she describes it, God appeared to her in a dream. God spoke to her and told her to "get up and care for these children." And he added, "You are not alone. I am with you every moment."

Gutti not only moved back to the village to care for her nieces and nephews, she set up a clinic to take care of other HIV-positive patients and their families. Eventually Gutti's brood grew to more than forty children, as other orphans joined the ranks of her "family." As the news spread, though, that Gutti was taking care of orphans, strangers began to leave their children on her doorstep, and eventually her simple clinic became over-whelmed with the sheer number of children for which she was caring. Soon she was forced to put up a sign turning families away. This broke Gutti's heart. She prayed for a miracle.

The miracle came in the form of other families who lived near Gutti and who had watched her living testimony. They did not want the orphaned children to be abandoned, so they started taking in the children themselves. Where Gutti could not help any longer, the neighbors stepped in. Finally, the community created a neighborhood orphanage, and one family after another provided shelter and care for those in need.

I sat with my mouth opened (but silent) while Gutti told her story. Though I had spoken to the crowd at the summit meeting the day before, my own story seemed so small and insignificant in comparison to what this woman shared. I know my story has power—God has shown that, but *the story is only about me*, I had thought. This story, this woman's life, was about *others*. She herself was just the crossroads where these stories came together.

"What caused you to give up everything and do this?" I finally blurted out.

"Compassion," she said strongly.

"Compassion?" I said. "That's all?"

"Oh, child," she replied in her stronger African accent. "That is enough."

When we looked up the word *compassion* in the dictionary, we discovered that compassion and acts of compassion are more than just feeling sorry for someone or simply stopping to meet his or her needs. The actual root of the word comes from a word that means literally to place yourself into the "shoes of the other person." You "take on their pain, their lostness, their struggle," so that you not only help them, you fully experience their struggle. This relationship changes the world. The real goal, and purpose, of compassion is not just one single act of kindness. It is a recasting of the situation so that kindness becomes the predominant frame for how a person moves forward from there.

As I looked in the Scripture, I found this focus over and over again, especially in the life of Jesus. Jesus, the Scripture stated, did not just see the needs of others or respond to those needs (though that is incredibly important, and something we will look at together later); he had "compassion" on them. Jesus left his home in heaven and became like us to "walk in our shoes" and to experience the full nature of our human existence—which we refer to as the Incarnation—so that what we felt, endured, and believed, he could experience firsthand as well.

Before the Incarnation, God, the Bible says, was "mindful" of our condition. With Jesus becoming like us, God became compassionate and walked with us. There is a dramatic difference.

Gutti changed me forever. I realized that my story was one thing, a tool that God had given me, but it was not enough in my following of his will. If I was to be all that God needed me to be, I had to get out of myself and "walk in the shoes" of my brothers and sisters. I had to experience and share real "compassion." Without it, I would remain at the fringes of what God was doing and could do through me. I wanted more. God wanted more. And that is why we want more for you.

Friend, these next ten days are about moving you out of your circumstances—maybe not literally, but certainly emotionally, intellectually, and spiritually, so that you can "put on the shoes" of those around you. That is God's plan for us—to become his compassion.

This part of the spiritual treatment plan focuses on the area of compassion in our lives—where we are getting it right, where we are missing the boat, and where God has something amazing and wonderful to show us, if only we will stop long enough to gather it in.

Before you start working on compassion, though, there are a couple of things to consider. First, during the next ten days God is going to place in your path both people who will champion you and people who will challenge you in the work of compassion. Don't be frustrated or resistant; this is all part of what God is doing. Remember, God has something better in store for you than the chronic life. He is changing your "normal." He is actively working in your life. This isn't just about another Bible study or devotional guide. God wants nothing more than to reshape you and your potential. And second, we want to be the first to pray for you, to ask that what you see and do over the next few days will be exactly what you need to begin the journey out of the chronic life. Oh, friend, we so want you to set down the worries and start watching for the wonders! You will not be the same if you do.

Let's pray:

Gracious God, we are ready to jump now—to jump out of our own troubles and baggage and into a conversation about how we can walk in the shoes of our brothers and sisters. We know it will not be easy. Protect us, we pray, as we make ourselves vulnerable to feel the power of real compassion and real incarnation through you. Amen.

RECOMMENDED RESOURCES

McKinley, Rick. *Jesus in the Margins.* Sisters, Ore.: Multnomah Books, 2005.
Warren, Rick. *The Purpose Driven Life.* Grand Rapids, Mich.: Zondervan, 2010.

TEN-DAY SPIRITUAL TREATMENT PLAN FOR COMPASSION

DAY ONE: WHEN LIFE NEEDS A TURNAROUND

Scripture: Read Haggai 1:3-6, 8-11.

DISCOVER

SHANE: The street where I live has a series of turn lanes that take you into one of the many cul-de-sacs in the neighborhood. My particular turn lane is nestled between a power company meter box and a row of crepe myrtle bushes that look a bit out of place where we live in Florida, since the rest of the street is lined with palm trees. It is rare (dare I say, almost never) that I turn down any other street but my own.

However, the other day my wife and I drove to the end of our parkway. We had lived in our neighborhood for almost a year and had never been to the end of the main road. We live in a nice but unspectacular subdivision with row after row of cul-de-sacs.

Eventually my wife—who, I must disclose, was not so keen on making this trip—advised me to turn around. But no lane allowed U-turns. So we drove on, looking for a sign that said a U-turn was permissible, or at least one area where the sign didn't say it wasn't. By what seemed like the fifteenth turn area or so, my wife encouraged me (as only spouses can) to "simply turn around."

"But it says 'no U-turns,'" I said.

"Honey," she replied, "we haven't seen a single car in over a mile. I think we can safely make a U-turn."

We made a U-turn at the next turn lane, against my better judgment, I might add. What a rash abandonment of the law!

But seriously, later I wondered why a street as long as our parkway would not have a place for a person to turn around. Then, it hit me: They wanted you to go to the very end, to see as many houses and subdivisions as possible.

Life feels like that road many times. It is long, unswerving, and there appears to be no place to turn things around.

But God works in a different way. Haggai says that God allows for course corrections. In essence, God allows for U-turns.

Maybe your life needs a U-turn today—a place, an occasion, an opportunity to stop going in that same direction that has led to so many problems, and to try something new.

The chronic life is often a pattern of no-turn lanes. But U-turns are exactly what we need in order to begin again and make a difference. As the Bible says, you can't go in two directions at once.

DEEPEN

In what areas of your life do you need a "U-turn"? What keeps you from making those changes? What would those changes look like in your life? How would you describe the "turnaround" God is looking for in Haggai 1:3-6, 8-11? What does Haggai say about stinginess?

How does Haggai's story reflect your journey? What can we learn from his advice and suggestions?

DEPLOY

Make a list of patterns and areas in your life in which you need to make a "U-turn." Write down a process for making the necessary changes, and include dates by which you plan to make these important changes happen. With whom will you need to work in order to accomplish these changes?

DISCERN

Pray: *Gracious God, forgive us when we go in directions that are not healthy for us. Thank you for giving us Jesus as the opportunity to make a U-turn and to start again. Amen.*

DAY TWO: MEET A GOD WHO IS INTERESTED IN YOU

Scripture: Read Zechariah 7:4-10.

DISCOVER

DEANNA: I have talked often about the first time my husband, Brett, and I met. We grew up in the same area in southern Mississippi, and I knew of his family. We liked each other from the beginning, though we never would have admitted it.

Brett has always been a risk taker. He loves to be outside and to do things (maybe to the extreme) that most guys like to do. Needless to say, he has never put a lot of thought into the ways of romance or courtship. And as a tomboy, that was "OK" by me.

The first time we went on a date, Brett convinced me to throw a baseball with him. His father looked outside and saw Brett throwing his best fastball with me acting as the catcher. Brett's father was horrified. He yelled, "Brett, don't you hurt that girl! What are you doing?" The reply was pure Brett: "Well, she's *catching* it." And I was.

The next time we were together, we decided to go swimming. Except Brett and his brother convinced me that to go swimming with them meant having to "pass the test"—which included jumping off the roof of the pool house, flying over the shallow end, and landing in the deep end of the pool. It is a wonder we survived!

But looking back, Brett and I have taken many "leaps" since then. I will never forget the day I realized how much this shy country boy liked me—a tough girl from the northern part of the county, someone more interested in basketball than dating. And yet I remember he made me smile, and this friendship felt special.

Did you know that God loves you even more than the person who loves you best on this earth, and that he is interested in what is happening in your life? With all that I have been through in my life, I am reminded that God not only loves me and wants the best for me, God is genuinely interested in whether my days are good and how my life is going.

So many people today believe they have no one, not even God. But God is not just some concept or a faraway figure on a mountain somewhere. Through Jesus, God has become like us, to live in us, and to make the "leaps" with us from the good and the not-so-good places of life. And the Bible says that no matter from where we jump, we are never alone.

DEEPEN

What do Zechariah's words say about God's intentions for how he wants us to treat one another? Reread verses 7:7-10. What commands does Zechariah list as God's plan for how we "model" God's love for us? How does this translate to your life and to your relationships? What "leaps of faith" does God need you to take in order to experience his "interest" in you? If God were telling you directly, "You are interested in religion, I am interested in people" (as Zechariah's words are paraphrased in *The Message*), what would he mean?

DEPLOY

Make a list of ways to show compassion in your life and in your community. Create a "comparison graph" whereby on one side of the paper you make a list of those activities that are about your own personal interests, and on the other side you list those activities that point others back to God.

DISCERN

Pray: *Gracious God, forgive us when we can't see others because of our selfish desires and needs. Help us leave behind our self-centered approach to life, so that we might find "real life" in you. Amen.*

DAY THREE: LIVING THE LOVE THAT GOD INTENDS

Scripture: Read John 17:20-23, 26.

DISCOVER

SHANE: The church I founded and served as senior pastor for ten years rested in the heart of a small south Mississippi community not known in prior years for its inclusiveness. I knew this going in, and thus, as the HIV-positive minister coming to town, I was anxious as to how I would be accepted.

To my surprise and delight, the town not only accepted me and my family, they allowed us to grow and experience one of the sweetest times of our lives and ministry.

The church we founded exhibited the desire of the community to be known for more than its personal history insisted. Our little congregation became a place where a variety of people worshiped, found fellowship, and were accepted into the life of the community. We had rich and poor, lost and found, broken and whole. Each Sunday was a new opportunity to see God's plan in action.

On one particular Sunday, I looked at the front door of the community center we had rented for worship, and I saw a picture that epitomized for me who these people were. A gentleman, just back from a long rehabilitation due to an accident that had led to the amputation of his left leg, was a in a wheelchair being pushed by another gentleman who had prosthetic legs from the knees down, the result of a long-ago hit-and-run by a drunk driver. As these two men approached the door, a young-adult woman with cerebral palsy moved to the door and opened it for them. She could not speak, and she had pronounced mobility issues. She also had the most beautiful smile.

That picture framed God's love. Two brothers, challenged by their wounds, assisted by a sister whom many in the world would ignore. What a beautiful image! What a beautiful place!

The Gospel of John speaks to Christ's love for us as more than a set of do's and don'ts but as expressions—pictures, if you will—of how that love is to look on a daily basis. Sometimes it looks a lot like the world, while at other times it looks more like the city gates and broken places, but nonetheless joyful and special.

Today, watch for those images of where God "shows off" his love for us the way he intended from the beginning. It is extravagant and exceptional to behold. Not only will you not be disappointed; you will be pleasantly, wholly surprised.

DEEPEN

What does it feel like to have Jesus praying for you? Does his prayer for unity among you and your brothers and sisters challenge you to live your life differently? What does the list in Jesus' prayer tell you about his love and his intentions for how we are to treat one another? In what ways should we become the model for how Christ's love in us should be pictured and experienced?

DEPLOY

Make a list of those qualities Jesus included in his prayer for his followers. Check off that list throughout the day. How many did you get right? How many need extra work? What does a faithful response to Jesus' prayer mean for us as we walk in faith together? If Jesus wants to have "one mind with you" and, thus, wants us to have one mind together as "he has with the Father," what does that mean for our day-to-day living of our faith?

DISCERN

Pray: *Gracious God, we know that we often miss the needs of others because we are distracted by our own needs and our troubles. Help us "walk out" of our internal view and watch for how you are working in the world, so that we may love others as you love us. Amen.*

DAY FOUR: LIVING WELL, LIVING BLESSED

Scripture: Read Mark 5:25-34.

DISCOVER

SHANE: Several years ago, a friend of mine arrived at my office utterly disheveled. I could tell that she was upset and that something horrible clearly had happened. But when I asked what was wrong, she would only say that she had fallen down some steps at work. The bruises on her leg and her torn skirt spoke to something else having taken place, but I knew that my friend was not talking.

Over several days, my wife and I took care of our friend. She stayed at our house and nursed her wounds (those on the outside) until she felt comfortable to talk about the ones on the inside.

When she did, we were stunned.

My friend finally shared that her boss (a person we knew well) had sexually harassed her. He had touched and groped her and held her in place by force. As our friend described the scene, at the moment the man was about to rape her, a member of the building's cleaning crew came into the office, having heard the commotion. Our friend gathered her things and left the office, but she accidentally left her purse.

What we did not know was that the man in question had devised this elaborate plan and a lie to cover it up, saying that our friend had made the advances on him. She would later say that she had been friendly to this man, and that the man understood what "no" meant and crossed that line anyway.

Over the next six months, we were embroiled in a sexual harassment suit between our friend and her boss. The man accused us of many things, saying that we had turned our backs on him and that, as his friends, too, we should have been more caring. We certainly cared about him. This was not the person we had grown to know. But the facts as he described them seemed difficult to believe: the man is well over six feet tall, and our female friend weighs barely over one hundred pounds.

Rumors flew back and forth that our female friend had been too provocative. "Maybe she brought this on herself," some people said. Nothing could have been farther from the truth, but it didn't keep people from speculating and gossiping. Because of this stress, there were times when our friend almost quit. She didn't see any other way. But she kept saying that if she didn't keep going, this man would do this to someone else. And so she persisted in her legal case. Finally, another woman came forward and admitted that the man had done the same thing to her. Then another woman came forward, and then another.

Our friend's courage to step out from the crowd, summon her strength, and go forward made the difference not only her in life, but also in the lives of others. In the story in Mark 5, the woman with the bleeding condition is an outcast, plain and simple. For no cause of her own, she is considered unclean and unholy. But after trying everything else, she heard that Jesus could make a difference. If she stepped out, people would talk, scoff; some would blame her for putting this Teacher into an awkward situation. But she believed in Jesus. And more important, Jesus believed in her. And so, she stepped from the crowd to touch the back of his garment, confident that would be enough to feel his power.

It was. And her life was never the same.

Sometimes, moving out of the chronic life is about courage—raw and irrational in the eyes of the world—but courage nonetheless. Sometimes we believe it is easier to keep our mouths shut, to shrink back from living justly and rightly in our walk. But God expects more from us. And God's people need more from us. To live as though just touching the hem of Jesus' clothes will alter your future may be the most illogical event to the world, but it is the most reasonable act in God's economy. God is waiting for you to step from the crowd and to stand up for something better. Being silent, keeping the status quo, being part of the group won't cut it any longer.

God pushes us out of our comfort zones that our lives might be changed. And in turn, we can change the world.

DEEPEN

What does Jesus' response to the woman with the bleeding condition tell us about his heart for those who are hurting? What impact did Jesus' knowing the woman's "whole story" have on the situation? Put yourself in her situation: describe how she felt, from the first part with her nervous awe, to the end, when Jesus confirms her faith. Now, tell Jesus the "whole story" about something in your life. How does it feel to lay that before Jesus and touch the hem of his grace?

DEPLOY

Find yourself a "prayer closet"—maybe not a real closet, but an area where you can be alone with Christ. Kneel, as the woman in Mark 5 did, and spend a few minutes soaking up Jesus as though he were standing in front of you. Write down your feelings and emotions about being so vulnerable before God. Now, repeat this process two other times during the day. If you can't kneel physically, find a place to sit and just be still before God. Finally, contact a friend and encourage this friend to take on a posture of living prayer as well. Set a date to share how God worked in both of your lives through these moments.

DISCERN

Pray: *Gracious God, give us the faith and the courage to follow where you lead us, to stand for what is right, to respond to those in need, to love unconditionally, and to forgive but not forgo what is redemptive. Help us be amazed by the extravagant nature of right living. Our proximity means everything. We are nothing without you. Amen.*

DAY FIVE: WHEN GOD HANDS OUT LIFE CHANCES

Scripture: Read Haggai 2:1-9.

DISCOVER

SHANE: One of my favorite teachers in high school was also one of my most challenging. The challenging teachers were the ones who gave the most homework and required the strictest detail for completing assignments. And they were the ones who expected the most from us when we left the classroom.

I was always a pretty good student, and I tried not to take my studies for granted. But not every subject came easy for me, and so to have teachers who cared about me meant a great deal.

I have heard a friend of mine who is a college professor say that "education is a society's process for handing out its life chances to people." I completely agree. I knew that getting a good education meant a lot, and no matter what else I was dealing with in my life, I was committed to finishing my studies.

DEANNA: As I mentioned earlier, most people know that Brett and I have been together most of our lives. And the road has not always been easy or smooth. From the outside looking in, other people's lives often look perfect or problem-free. But the truth is, all of us face struggles and personal challenges of our own. Brett and I feel blessed to have carried each other through the storms of life, through both the difficult times and the good times, and it is through faith and love that we have supported each other and grown stronger together as a couple.

In our early years, before our marriage, Brett worked to get his NFL career off the ground, while I worked odd jobs, went to school, and lived as a single mother. It was certainly a struggle, but I was committed to getting my education and making it on my own, if need be.

Certainly, now, God has blessed us. But I wouldn't trade those moments or my education for anything. It was my "life chance," and it gave me the strength and courage to know that, if I needed to, I could make it on my own.

SHANE: As Deanna's story shows, our "life chances" are more than just the opportunities afforded to us. They are also the opportunity for how we can help others. The more skilled, prepared, resourced, and aware we are, the better we respond to the needs of those around us. Our life chances become the life chance for someone else.

I believe God's love for us is our spiritual life chance. And we are called to accept it for ourselves but then to use that love to become Christ's example in the way we treat one another. God has so many wonderful gifts for us, and even better, the Scriptures say that he is pleased and excited to give them to us (see Galatians 1). It is his source of joy to participate in the life of his children and to offer them a new way, a better way to experience life.

We have watched teachers light up when they see that glimmer in a student's eye or that confidence in his or her once-shaky voice. This is why they do what they do—for the love of handing out "life chances." God is the cosmic model of this example. He "delights" in loving us. Can anything be sweeter than that?

As Haggai states, all that God expects is for us to approach him faithfully and to respond affirmatively to what he offers. He will guide us in the rest—the details, the rules, the boundaries. Our job is to follow. God leads the way. Don't be timid, my friend, in taking on the blessing that God so graciously wants to give you. It is your birthright, your privilege, your life chance.

DEEPEN

Haggai says that God is waiting to provide us a blessing that, if accepted, will change our futures. First, what does that blessing mean to you? And what keeps us from responding to God's call or offer? Second, why is it so important to God that we work and respond boldly once we have decided to accept that gift? What does it say about both the value of what God is offering and God's own feelings about providing this gift for his children?

DEPLOY

Get some molding clay. Using your creativity and imagination, use the clay to shape symbols of the issues that keep you from living a whole and holy life. Now, how would God re-mold those obstacles for you? Make a list of ways in which you can help "shape" someone else's connection to God. Also, think of a friend whose life lacks meaning and purpose and who would benefit from Haggai's reminder that God owns the gold and silver and is just as capable of providing all we need.

DISCERN

Pray: *Gracious God, it is easy for us to simply let life slip by without becoming all that you have in store. But you expect us to get out of our own way and to take on the principles of your love and grace. We want to be shaped by you and sent by you. We love you. Amen.*

DAY SIX: WHEN GOD IS ON THE MOVE

Scripture: Read Zechariah 2:1-5, 10-13.

DISCOVER

SHANE: The first neighborhood my wife and I lived in was a closed, stand-offish community. The neighbors were courteous but not overly so. My wife is such a people person, though, that she literally loved them out of their homes and made friends with most everyone on the street. And yet when someone new would move in, the neighborhood reverted back to its old patterns, with the established residents making the new folks "earn their place," as one person remarked.

It was very difficult to watch this happen, because I knew that not everyone responded the same way my wife did, and that a lot of the new neighbors would simply retreat behind the blinds of their homes and never really get to know anyone. I was also disappointed for our neighborhood, because every time we thought we "had it" and were moving forward, we seemed to back up three steps.

This wonderful passage from Zechariah 2 is one of the most vivid in Scripture. The image of God standing ready to measure the walls of Jerusalem as a way to verify God's promise he would never leave is profound. But all the more profound is when God says that not only will I protect you by becoming that "wall of protection" in your life, but I am also moving into your neighborhood: "I will protect you, yes, but I also plan to live among you."

What an incredible image, for the God of the universe to move into our neighborhood and to set up residence where we are. But that has been God's M.O. from the beginning, and it is the frame for what *Immanuel* ("God with Us") really means.

Our challenge is to watch for God's work and movement, and to be ready when God is up to something spectacular. You can bet that it will pull you from your daily grind, bring you into fellowship with your brothers and sisters, and most likely, change your world. We simply must trust God to protect our comings and goings, and thus everything else in between.

DEEPEN

Zechariah says that God is building a perimeter around Jerusalem to protect and to guide. How does that image correspond with what God has promised to do in our lives? In what areas of your life do you need an extra ounce of protection and wisdom? Zechariah also says that God is moving into our neighborhoods, close to the ones God loves. How does that act of fellowship from God warm our hearts and then teach us to treat others? We have more than a command to love and be in fellowship with one another; we have a model from God.

DEPLOY

Get to know your neighbors. Do something to be in fellowship with those who live and work near you, and give them time to respond to your kindness and hospitality.

DISCERN

Pray: *God, when you moved into our neighborhood, you transformed our present and our future. We were not created to make this journey alone. Give us the heart to feel your presence, the words to speak of your love, the courage to reach out in need, and the wisdom to watch for those who are broken. Amen.*

DAY SEVEN: REAL FRIENDS

Scripture: Read John 14:15-17.

DISCOVER

DEANNA: When I was informed that I had breast cancer, I remember the sensation of knowing that there was something inside of me that was doing harm to my body. It was like the cancer became its own living entity, the monster hiding under the bed. In fact, for a few days, it was all I could think about as I got my mind around what this meant for me, my family, and our future.

However, a friend of mine, who came by the house to drop off casseroles and get-well notes and gifts, could tell that I was struggling with this new-found diagnosis. I shared with my friend my feelings of not being able to outrun whatever this was inside of me, and the fear and doubt it caused.

My friend said, "Sure, you have cancer inside your body, but you also have Christ." I will never forget those words. They were simple, to the point, and incredibly true. To know that whatever we were facing inside our bodies, or our life, God is right there living in us too, ready to protect and care for us from the inside out.

My friend's words were comforting because I had forgotten that I had someone much stronger and bigger than cancer living within me, and that God would be my refuge and my source of strength.

But it does not stop there. As John 14 states, the goal is to then share what God has placed inside you with those around you. This is one gift that you want to give away.

Disease and illness may permeate our bodies, but God promises that they cannot permeate our souls and spirits unless we let them. And to help in the fight, Scripture says that God has given us the Holy Spirit, a Friend, to go along on the journey with us and to help us help others make the steps as well.

DEEPEN

John talks about a friend whom God has given to us. Who is that friend, and why does that gift mean so much to our relationship with God? God's goal in this passage is to encourage us to live more like God and to share love with those around us. Why does God offer us a friend to assist us in the process and the journey? When the Scripture says that "the "godless world can't take him in because it doesn't have eyes to see him" (verse 17 *The Message*), why is that important for us in drawing close to God through the Holy Spirit?

DEPLOY

Make a list of some of your friends today. What qualities do you love most in them? How do you see those qualities in your relationship with God?

DISCERN

Pray: *Father and Friend, we cannot understand the grace we have been offered until we have been able to step out of our own shoes and walk in the shoes of others. Help us set down our struggles and take up the gift and blessing of what you offer in Christ. We love you. Amen.*

DAY EIGHT: THE ONE OTHER THING

Scripture: Read Mark 10:17-22.

DISCOVER

SHANE: People loved asking Jesus questions. Why wouldn't they? He was open, approachable, respected. His demeanor provided acceptance to just about everyone who came to him, whether it was a Pharisee or a common person from the dusty streets. Jesus loved people—and he loved talking to them about their ideas, conditions, and solutions. Yes, it was easy to ask questions of Jesus.

But people did not necessarily like Jesus' answers. They were a different bag. Though Jesus encouraged openness and acceptance, he also spoke the truth, was honest in his replies, and provided, sometimes to his own detriment, the most straightforward of responses, even on the most delicate of topics.

Some who came to Jesus walked away with a sense of justification and strength. Others strolled away burdened by the thought of how far they were from being able to live what he had just offered and encouraged. All left very different than before.

The real gifts of Jesus' responses were that he spoke about real significance and answers in a world that so often asks meaningless questions. Jesus would never settle for telling you what you wanted to hear, but he would most certainly share with you what you need. The gap between these two offered times of great joy and affirmation, but also great anxiety and disappointment. As Jesus said, the "truth will set you free" (see John 8:32) but many times freedom has a price.

Take one rich young man's encounter with Jesus, for instance. In the familiar account of the rich young ruler (see Mark 10), Jesus encounters a young man who believes he has all the rules of life in order. According to the standards of the young man's world, he probably did. We assume by

Mark's description that he was a good man, with position, title, and also enough spiritual maturity that he came to Jesus to ask what to him was an important question: "Good Teacher, what should I do to get eternal life?" (verse 14). We all have asked such questions, and in such ways as to get the answer we want, but not the one we necessarily need.

Jesus gave the latter. Jesus sensed that the young man was a good, noble person, so he said to keep the commandments. To which the young man replied, "I have done just that." The young man seemed proud of his reply and happy that he was headed down the right path. Who wouldn't be? He had just given the right answer to the right man. I am sure the young man stopped to look around, maybe even to peer at his neighbors and colleagues to make sure they heard his exchange with Jesus. All seemed right.

Then, at the end of their discussion, just as the young man was about to turn and leave, Jesus asked "one other thing." Oh, how I hate the "one other thing." When I was younger and got into trouble, I could usually talk myself out of most jams. But my mother, who was wise to my verbal acrobatics and keen debating skills (or, at least, the ones I had built up in my mind), would always give me enough room to feel that I was about to "win" the conversation . . . until the "one other thing." This "one other thing" would have to do with the piece of information I had left out of the story or the words left unsaid or the intention that I had not fully disclosed. No matter what or who or where the "one other thing" was, it was the very thing that was usually my downfall.

Of course, we know the end of the story and the impact Jesus' "one other thing" had upon this young man. Jesus said to him, in effect, "OK then, you have kept the commandments. But there's one other thing: go and sell all you have, and give it to the poor."

"What did he just say?" one of the bystanders must have whispered. I am sure the rich young ruler was thinking this as well. *Sell . . . give . . . poor?* The Scripture says that the story ends with the young man turning away "sadly" (verse 22), because . . . *one other thing* . . . he was very rich. The young man wanted more; he wanted significance. But significance requires "one other thing." Significance always has a price.

Many of us are unwilling to pay that price, to confront the "one other thing." But that "one other thing" is the line in the sand, and the means by which we encounter God's next step for grace and significance.

Are you willing to pay that price of the "one other thing"? Are you ready for that next step? Such is the difference between simple survival and true significance.

DEEPEN

What do you see in this story about the rich young ruler that reminds you of yourself or your own situation? What is different? What is the difference between the "morally good" about which the young man is talking and the "one other thing" that Jesus mentions? What things must be let go of in your life in order for you to see the deeper side of the Kingdom? What keeps you from achieving these things or beginning these changes? (Try to be specific in your self-assessment.)

DEPLOY

Make a list of those "moral" qualities that you believe you get right on a daily basis. How would Jesus refer to those qualities you listed? Now, make a list of the way you believe Jesus would call someone "good" or "moral." How is that list different? How could you live that difference today in your family, your parenting, your finances, your church life, and so forth?

DISCERN

Pray: *Gracious God, help me see the difference between "morally good" and what it really means to follow you in the world. Help me love and live faithfully like you because of who you are, not just because it is the right thing to do. I want to be like you, God. Make it so. Amen.*

DAY NINE: THE SOLID ROCK

Scripture: Read Psalm 62:1-2.

DISCOVER

We have heard the story of friends, a couple, who recently built a house. In fact, they built two houses. The house they live in now is their dream house. It is beautiful and tailored to their family's needs. It has a wonderful wrap-around porch, high ceilings, and a gorgeous stone fireplace that takes your breath away when you see it.

Not long ago, these friends had an open house and a gathering to celebrate their new home. It was the first time many present had been in that *particular* house, but not the first time they had been in that place.

What are we talking about? Well, just three years earlier, this same couple had built the exact same house plan with the same porch, ceilings, and fireplace, but in a different location. They gathered for the open house for that house too, but unbeknownst to them, cracks were forming in the foundation and the walls.

Within days of the party, the cracks had gone across the entire width of the house. Next, the floors developed uneven edges in the concrete, and the sheetrock literally tore from the studs in one room. It was like an earthquake was hitting the house in slow motion.

The couple called their builder, who came immediately. He was astonished at what he saw. The house he had spent so much time building was coming apart before his very eyes. But the builder knew exactly what was happening: the foundation was shifting.

He arranged for a soil test on the property. What the survey found was a vast landfill underneath not only the house, but under the entire neighborhood. The developer of the property, a well-respected man with a long history in the community, had gotten into serious financial trouble. When he realized he had purchased a parcel of land for a new development that was nothing but "shifting sands," or at the least, garbage, he was on the verge of losing everything.

Instead of telling the builders about the unstable land, he sold the lots without informing them. The builders, who had dealt with this man for many years, trusted his word that the properties were solid. In hindsight, everyone agreed that they should have gotten soil surveys for the property. They knew that unstable foundations lead to unstable construction, which leads to dangerous outcomes. Many of the homeowners and builders of this neighborhood, including our friends, involved themselves in a long legal process that led to the bankruptcy of not only the developer, but several of the local builders themselves. And no one recovered the full amount of his or her investment. In so many ways, it was an avoidable tragedy.

And so, a group of friends stood in this new house to celebrate a new home. But guests couldn't help thinking about the subtle but important differences in the two houses. Though they looked alike in so many ways, they were different in the *one* way that mattered the most: the second home sat on a solid foundation.

The psalmist tells us that God is our rock, our solid foundation. Without him we can build our lives and make them look as pretty as we like. But eventually, the cracks will come and the damage will be done. Jesus repeats this analogy in one of his most famous parables. Building our lives on "shifting sands" leads to broken hearts and devastated relationships.

But if we build our lives on Christ, we not only have the right foundation, we have the range to grow and build beyond our wildest imaginations a life that only God could design.

DEEPEN

Think for a moment about "where your life is built." What are the qualities of your life that are stable and sure? Why do you consider them "solid"? How does the Scripture passage teach us about growing deeper in our faith, by building from a solid foundation? What happens when we build on unstable surfaces in our lives? in our relationships? in our dreams?

DEPLOY

Go out and pick up several rocks. Hold them in your hands. What do they feel like? Why would the psalmist call God our solid "rock"? Make a list of the most important relationships in your life, and give them a stability rating between 1 and 10 (with 10 being the most solid and stable). How can you make the less stable relationships stronger? How do you protect and care for those that are doing well?

DISCERN

Pray: *Jesus, our solid Rock, thank you for being the foundation for our lives, our hopes, our dreams, and our futures. Help us stand firm on your love and grace, that we may build relationships that will weather the storms and stand the test of time. Amen.*

DAY TEN: COME ALONG WITH ME

Scripture: Read Matthew 9:9-13.

DISCOVER

SHANE: In my book *You Can't Do Everything . . . So Do Something,* I wrote about an encounter my daughter Emma Leigh and I had while visiting the city of New Orleans on a daddy-daughter day trip several years ago. Her comment when seeing a group of men and women who were living under the interstate overpass, was, "Do they belong to us?" It sounds like an odd question, but not to a three-year-old child trying to make sense of why the people living under the bridge had nowhere to go. It was a couple of years after Hurricane Katrina had ravaged the city, and although many volunteer service groups had made life a little more bearable for the masses of homeless who call New Orleans their own, the underpasses of Interstate 10 were still filled with those who had no other place to go. One part, in particular, is prolific with those living in such conditions. This is the Canal Street exit. As soon as you turn off of the interstate, you stop at a traffic light. On either side, behind you and in front of you, are people living in cardboard boxes, under blankets, and some out in the elements—all living in a makeshift city under the underpass.

I had noticed the scene before, but on that day I was surprised by the number of homeless persons there. Emma Leigh saw them too. She was three years old at the time, and although she was still a baby in so many ways, she had the vocabulary of a child much older, largely due to her having older sisters who included and involved Emma Leigh in almost every make-believe world they created. As she and I drove along, I adjusted my rearview mirror to watch her eyes. That is when she asked, "Daddy, who are they?" I explained that the men and women under the bridge didn't have homes, and that they were living the best way they knew. It was then that Emma Leigh stunned me: "Why don't their mommies and daddies come get them?" she asked. In her little world, everyone has mommies and daddies who take care of their children. I wondered how many of the people we were seeing now had wished the same thing.

I explained to Emma Leigh that many of them no longer had a family or that they couldn't get in touch with their family, or that for some of them, their family members were mad at them or they were mad at their families. I could tell in her eyes that this did not make sense. All she knew was a family who loved her very much, and who would go anywhere to take care of her and to make sure that she was OK. In fact, only a few weeks prior to that trip, she had called me at the office and had been tired and upset. "Can you come get me, Daddy?" she asked. "Of course I can," I replied. When she needed her daddy, he showed up. That is what daddies and mommies and families do. In fact, she had a whole host of people in her life who would respond. If for some reason she couldn't have gotten me, she certainly would have contacted her grandmothers or her aunt.

But to have *no one*; this did not compute for Emma Leigh, and I could tell that she did not know what to do with this idea. After a few beats, she replied, "That's OK. They can go live with their friends." Once again, in Emma Leigh's world, friends took care of each other. Then, as though she was ready for what my answer might be to that, she replied, "Or call their church." Now it was getting personal and painful, and I knew that at some point, this three-year-old would make too much sense, even for this situation.

Again, I tried to explain that their situations were difficult, and that they may not have friends who could or would help. That didn't seem to sit well with Emma Leigh either. She sat there for a second while I kept wondering why the traffic light was taking so long to change. Finally, feeling the need to say something, I blurted out, "They just don't 'belong' to anyone, sweetheart."

It was at that moment that my three-year-old daughter got the best of me. Jesus' calculations to his disciples that they should approach the Father as a child meant something in that moment, and I, for one, confronted it firsthand.

"Don't they belong to *us*, Daddy?" she finally responded. This was my three-year-old daughter's way of asking, *Aren't we their friends?* She didn't say anything else; she didn't need to.

The world's great weakness is that so many people believe (and, by our actions, we agree) that they belong to no one. Nothing could be farther from the truth. Jesus' ministry proved the opposite. He lived the opposite. Just ask Matthew, Zacchaeus, the woman caught in adultery—they found that, indeed, they belonged to Someone who would not let them down. No, it is their brothers and sisters who fail them, when we, by our piety, prejudice, or pride believe that we sit above or apart from others.

The family of God is united by deeper principles, Jesus taught us, than simply bloodlines. We are family because God made us so. "Come along with me" was not just an invitation to a local tax collector; it was *the* invitation, the reminder from the Creator of the universe that our home is with God and that we are never forgotten.

DEEPEN

Think about these words from Jesus in this Scripture passage: "I'm after mercy, not religion" (Matthew 9:13 *The Message*). What do these mean for those of us who are in the church? What does it offer for those far from God?

Have you ever felt like an outsider or someone who had been forgotten? How did it feel? How did it shape your view of yourself, others, and God? Have you ever made someone else feel that way? Why would we do that?

What are the "under the bridge" moments or situations you've seen or become aware of in your community? How does God wish you to respond to the needs of others around you?

DEPLOY

Decide on a "come along" moment in each day of your week. How can you touch another person's life (someone who is under-resourced or under-loved) and make a difference in his or her world?

DISCERN

Pray: *Dear Jesus, our Example and constant Friend, forgive us when we pass you by under the bridges of our lives. Help us see the faces of those in need all around us and not miss those whom you place in our path to remind us of your love and grace. In Jesus' name we pray. Amen.*

CHAPTER FOUR

THE CURE: UNDERSTANDING

A college professor friend, whose job it is to teach teachers, constantly provides new ways for educators to help people learn. There is always a new theory, philosophy, drill, or tool our friend is sharing that confounds us with its simplicity and success.

Teachers today are some of the most important people in our society, if not *the* most important. They are, as our friend likes to say, "the folks who make every other profession possible." That is a beautiful way to describe what is oftentimes an overlooked or underappreciated profession. Teachers are the doorways for a transformed life for our children. Education is, as some educators have insisted for generations, the missing link when it comes to economic prosperity and civil societies.

It is easy to see their point, especially when you look at societies where education is not a high priority or where educational opportunity is held back for many of its people. And when education is used for other purposes, such as class or wealth distribution, or for indoctrination of religious priorities or intolerance, the consequences can be devastating.

But in those places where education is fundamental and appreciated, you will find a core of dedicated people, teachers, administrators, and parents, whose lives surround the purpose of helping children discover their "life chance" and making the most of it.

Several years ago Howard Gardner, a Harvard educator who works with brain-based research and design, detailed how the real question for education is not "How smart are you?" but rather, *"How* are you *smart?"* There is a critical difference in these questions.

For years, we have fed into the model of testing-and-response very well. Those who are good students by the standards used to measure aptitude for certain subjects, such as writing, math, history, and so on, tested well and fit within the model for what learning was believed to be at its best. But we knew friends who handled none of those topics very well. In fact, some of these friends were in the learning disabled class and made to take remedial steps for even the most basic of topics. They unfairly were considered by some to be "not too bright."

But one friend in particular knew how to take a car engine apart without consulting a book and using only his bare hands. He could then, again without help, put the engine back together. He was and is a master of things that run, of engines, and of those arts that many of us take for granted every time we put our key into the ignition. Our friend finally finished high school, but no one took much notice. Where is he today? He owns a successful mechanics business and has done very well for his family, though many would still consider him "unlearned" because he would not do well on any of the standardized measures for intelligence. Trust us, these friends are incredibly smart, just not in the ways we like to describe.

Our college professor friend says that many people become confused about the topic of education because they focus on knowledge and the process for acquiring it, rather than really working to help people "learn." "There is a monumental difference," she will say in her seminars. "Knowledge is a snapshot of information—here today, gone tomorrow, especially if it is not needed." But she will always add, "Learning is about a changed life, about transformation. When people learn something, it changes the other parts of them, and they are never the same again."

This is also true in our spiritual lives. There are some things that we learn very early in life; or at least it is *better* if we learn them early. Nothing substitutes for taking our children to church or for helping them to know their Bibles and learn how to pray. George Barna's research suggests that over 75 percent of people who come to know Christ as their Savior in any given year will do so between the ages of five and thirteen (see the Barna Group's website at www.barna.org). That is the most fertile time and place in a young person's life for taking the principles of Christ and allowing them to guide him or her, to become part of daily life. But, for instance, how much money does a church usually spend on children's ministries? Not much in comparison to how much we spend on keeping the church's lights on or the piano in the sanctuary tuned.

What most people experience of faith is, unfortunately, about knowledge. They have taken in snapshots on their way to being influenced by every other thought pattern, philosophy, or theory the world can throw at them. What we really need is "learning"—about the love and grace of God, about the Word of God in action, and about the power of being the "hands and feet of Jesus" every day. Not only will our lives change, but it will change our world.

And these are not just the opinions of those of us who are pro-intellect and pro-education. The apostle Paul says that we should not be conformed by the world, but we should be transformed in the gospel by the "renewing of our minds." We have to "unlearn" all of those "snapshots" that we have been taught and get back to real learning, real life change as intended by God.

The chronic life shuts off our ability to assimilate the new ways in which God is working in our lives. "When the world becomes about us," one of our friends likes to say, "we start living in a spiritual, emotional, relational, and intellectual black hole, unable to take in the ever-present, ever-engaging Good News of Jesus." Jesus told his disciples, "go and make disciples of all the nations" (Matthew 28:19)—a process that, in the Hebrew or Greek worlds, required time spent under the mentoring of a trusted master— "baptizing them. . . . **Teach** [them] to obey all the commands I have given you" (verses 19-20, emphasis added). Nothing substitutes, either in Jesus' or Paul's mind, for good, faithful religious instruction. The more we know of God's Word, the more we know of God's world. The more we know of God's world, the more we can follow God's will. It is that simple.

But *understanding* is not just intellectual in nature. It also involves taking the time to understand our brothers and sisters, what drives them, what keeps them up at night. We will have a new glimpse of these questions and answers once we spend some time in their shoes, but when we expand the conversation, not only will we broaden our scope of their situation, but we also will be more prepared for how the next curve in the road over which God sends us looks and works.

The chronic life is about keeping us *in the dark* and *out of the know* for as long as spiritually possible. When this happens, we become facsimiles of ourselves, copied and pasted into place without much purpose or any real means for making life mean something more. The more we understand of God's world and God's children, the more we actually "learn" about ourselves. And true to form, the experience is life changing.

Over the next ten days, we will spend time focusing on *understanding*. By now, God has already sent people into your life on whom you have placed your hat of compassion. You have walked in their shoes and know the pain and struggle they feel. Now is the time to broaden the scope and spend some time learning where God wants you to move next. This will require some real effort, some real work. It won't be easy. But keep in mind that it is not about "how smart you are" in terms of your spiritual aptitude; it is about "*how* smart are you." Ask yourself: how has God gifted you to take what you have learned, put that together with what is already deep inside of you, and go and change your world? The results will be no less than profound.

As we move into this next section of the spiritual treatment plan, we encourage you and remind you that God is sending people into your journey. This is not a "snapshot" for God; he wants nothing less than to change your life, so that you can change others. We pray that God will continue to amaze you and that he will, by the renewing of your mind, change your heart.

Let's pray:

Gracious God, we have spent ten days watching the world from a new angle, from a new point of view, with a focus on compassion. We want not only to know compassion; we want to live it. Thank you for sending those people into our lives who have caused us to move beyond our own needs and desires and to see the world with your eyes.

But now, God, we want to renew our minds. We want to understand, not simply in intellectual terms, but from the inside out. We want to know our brothers and sisters, the way they feel, the way you feel when you see them. Help us study your Word, as though we are facing the test of our life the next morning, and to pray as though we are calling out an S.O.S. from a deserted island. Lord, we don't want simply to catch a glimpse of you from the back of your robe. No, we want to jump into the middle of the conversation and be caught by you, and thus be changed. We love you, God. Amen.

RECOMMENDED RESOURCES

Hybels, Bill. *Axiom: Powerful Leadership Proverbs*. Grand Rapids, Mich.: Zondervan, 2008.

Lewis, C. S. *Mere Christianity*. San Francisco: HarperSanFrancisco, 2001.

TEN-DAY SPIRITUAL TREATMENT PLAN FOR UNDERSTANDING

DAY ELEVEN: HOW DO YOU DEFINE *QUALITY*?

Scripture: Read Psalm 34:1-9.

DISCOVER

SHANE: I serve a congregation that has seven worship services on the weekends over three church campuses. These worship services cover the spectrum of worship styles, from traditional/liturgical to very casual contemporary.

When I first arrived at this congregation, I could tell that there was a strain between those who attended one service or another. Each group spoke of the other attendees as though they were part of another congregation instead of belonging to the same church.

Nowhere was this more evident than in the 9:30 A.M. Sunday worship service at what had been the first of our campuses. That service was and remains the largest worship service of all seven and has a long history in the life of our church. It is contemporary, not as much so as the "contemporary" worship service at many churches, but still more so than a traditional United Methodist service.

As I would talk with people about worship (one of my most important topics, and one I addressed first), people on both sides of the issue *always* had an opinion. It was striking. This worship service had been in existence for many years (probably more than two decades) and had the same leadership for the last ten years. But for members of the congregation, both this worship service's attendees and those who attend other services, to continue to have such emotion about a worship experience seemed very strange.

I have seen this before while consulting in churches. Those who attend the traditional services sometimes get upset over the "new," more contemporary worship service, which usually starts at an earlier hour and is held in the gym or fellowship hall, because they feel that it has taken away all "the young families." And yet, to have a service that was so successful for so long still generate comments such as "It is the time slot" or "They don't feel like they belong to the rest of the church" was troubling.

The more investigation I did into the history of the service, though, I discovered that there was a back story to the conversation; there always is. The 9:30 A.M. service was created a couple of decades ago because the church had run out of space. This service was started, originally, as a traditional worship service, very much like the style of the current 11:00 A.M. worship service. However, in the mid-1990s, amid the rush to modernize and offer options in worship, a small group of church members convinced the pastor at the time to transition the style. Literally, one Sunday morning the service was traditional in style, and the next Sunday morning it was contemporary. And the rest, as they say, is history.

Those who had attended the 9:30 A.M. service but preferred the traditional style felt betrayed, and those who had craved something new and saw that new people were drawn by this style felt vindicated by the change.

Over the years, very little had been done to help the two groups talk past discussions about reaching "seekers" and those "far from God." The result was a contentiousness that existed and grew in the life of the congregation over worship styles, creating a basic mistrust that must, at his heart, wound God very much.

In Psalm 34:1-9, the psalmist describes worship in different terms. There is no mention either of liturgy or being modern in his description.

There is no mention of a worship committee or even a strategy for how to reach those outside the worship family. Quite the contrary, here the psalmist spends most of his time talking about the family itself, and how important it is to be united and together, similar themes to Jesus' own prayers some eight hundred years later.

The psalmist understood something that most of us miss: that worship is not about us. It never was intended to be about us. Instead, worship is solely about God—God's presence, God's Spirit, God's worth and greatness, and God's response in our lives. When we worship, the psalmist would suggest, *we* get a chance, a gift in being in God's presence, not the other way around—and we receive this gift regardless of the particular style of worship.

According to Scripture, the precepts for good worship are much the same whether we worship as a group or as individuals. It is about being present with God, keeping our hearts and spirits focused on God's movement in, about, and through us, and then responding faithfully to whatever he asks and does in us.

I love the phrase "open your mouth and taste, open your eyes and see—how good God is" (Psalm 34:8 *The Message*). That is the purpose of worship. The psalmist concludes that verse, "Blessed are you who run to him," and that holds true whether you are hearing the organ or the drums while doing so.

The last verse of this passage is telling for churches as we prepare our worship experiences. So many of us are seeking excellence and significance in our ministries. We are seeking the same for our lives. But the psalmist makes it simple: "Worship God if you want the best; worship opens doors to all his goodness" (verse 9 *The Message*). Worship is the way we understand God. And if we are to understand our world, it helps to spend time understanding the Creator first. Many of us miss this part in our spiritual journey. We forget that God has "opened the Book" to us so that we might see the story from his point of view. From there, we catch a glimpse of so many angles and places where God works in our lives. Want to confront the chronic life? Begin by confronting the real story of how it should have unfolded in the first place. That "understanding," as the psalmist says, is "worth more than gold."

DEEPEN

Describe your current worship experiences. What makes them significant, or in what ways are they lacking in your life right now? What changes could you make in how you approach worship that would change the power of what you experience? The psalmist says that if we "want the best," we should worship. How does worship usher in the best in our relationships with God? How does worship, as the psalmist says, "open doors to goodness"? What does "goodness" mean for you and your life?

DEPLOY

Keep a "worship journal," in which you describe the experiences of worship and of meeting God in your life. Reflect: How does God work in and through you during worship?

DISCERN

Pray: *Gracious God, we want to open the doors of our hearts and lives, and be amazed at your presence. Show us something of your heart today that propels us past our preconceived notions of what worship should be to see a new and more powerful view of you. Amen.*

DAY TWELVE: CAN'T WE ALL GET ALONG?

Scripture: Read Malachi 2:5-10.

DISCOVER

DEANNA: The world remembers the media circus that ensued with our transition from Green Bay, the meetings with team officials, the conversations about staying out of football, and then, eventually, Brett's trade to the New York Jets in 2008. By the end of the process, we were exhausted from the tension in our relationships with people we loved and respected. We felt the strain from people's perceptions and wished that we could just shout what we really felt and believed, though we knew that was impossible and probably still would not do much good. The result was a difficult break from Green Bay that not only affected those of us directly involved but disappointed a fan base that we love so much.

I love this passage from Malachi because it is so real. God has made a covenant with the people, and when the people act according to God's standards, they exhibit the best of that relationship. But when they go their own way, the real brokenness of their lives shows through and, as Malachi notes, we see the real nature of their intentions.

People are like that today, too. Too often we create personas or perceptions that we want people to believe and see. But at the end of the day, it comes back to relationships and the integrity of people to live what they value. Things will be fine, the prophet says, as long as the current is smooth, but when the rough waters come, a person's real nature will surface.

When this happens to Malachi, he asks, in effect, "Can't we all just get along?" In essence, he is asking, "Have you forgotten what you said to each other earlier? Have you forgotten our former lives?"

But often, we do forget our "former lives," and we get so focused on the issues at hand that we forget how our relationships together have formed us and made us friends. For instance, people might assume that being traded or moving to a different sports team is just another business decision. But that's not the case. In sports, as in life, you build bonds and friendships that last forever. And transitions, no matter whether they take place in your local neighborhood or in the NFL, mean something and have an effect. No matter the situation, our goal is to live what we value and to be an example of how God's love guides us all.

When God's children act in a way that teaches the precepts of God's message faithfully, many people will see the goodness of God. When God's children act in the opposite way—well, you get the picture. That is why it is so important to protect our relationships at any cost. They are the picture we paint of our faith in action. If we fail to secure real purpose and focus in our lives, the misguided priorities will seep in and take over, and before long, we will wonder how we even arrived at such a place.

But a life lived faithfully to values, consistent in our objectives, and at peace with our relationships will find God's presence. And the better part of our nature, the part with God's imprint, will be evident to all.

DEEPEN

Malachi uses the example of the priest to discuss how we are to help God's people live faithfully in relationship with God and one another. What are the qualities of a priest? Describe the work of a priest in drawing us close to God. Describe the work of a priest in drawing us close to one another. In what ways can we mess up enough to create a broken example for others that it infects their own relationship with God and with God's people? Do you have situations and circumstances in your life that need adjustment in order to better testify to the goodness of God? In what ways could you help God's people "get along" instead of pulling apart?

DEPLOY

Make a list of those broken relationships where you need healing. Now, ask yourself what keeps you from seeking reconciliation and restoration. What one step could you take today that would begin that process in your life?

DISCERN

Pray: *Gracious God of peace, we confess that we have not always loved the way you have asked us to love. Forgive us where we have failed to be your people together, and help us restore our broken relationships. Amen.*

DAY THIRTEEN: PRAYING WITH A PURPOSE

Scripture: Read Matthew 6:5-13.

DISCOVER

SHANE: Our high school football coach was very successful as both a coach and a "life coach" for the young men who crossed his path. Being a hemophiliac, I could not play football because of the contact nature of the sport, but most of my friends played, and thus I wanted to be out there too. Therefore, I went to trainers' school and learned to be a sports medicine assistant for the team. That way, I could be a part of the team without endangering my health.

Our coach was gruff, silent, and very focused. When he was angry, you knew it by his steely stare and clinched jaw. When he was excited, well, it was hard to tell, because he rarely allowed himself to show any emotion.

But he was certainly a good man who loved the sport of football, and more important, he loved the kids he coached. And that relationship showed on the scoreboard. Our football teams were some of the most successful in our area, and our coach won numerous awards for his teams' abilities and achievements.

There was an unwritten rule about our coach. Most of the time, he said little and expected us to study our playbooks, know our jobs, and execute them to the best of our abilities. But if he had to *tell* us how to do something, we should consider it extremely important. And if he actually *showed* us how to do something, we should consider it sacred.

In Matthew 6:5-13, Jesus "shows" the disciples how to pray. They had asked earlier about praying deeper, focusing their hearts closer to God, but for one reason or another, they didn't seem to get it. Jesus didn't just tell them about prayer and its importance, he said, "Pray like this." And he showed the disciples through the Lord's Prayer how to do it.

The Lord's Prayer is many things, but Jesus never intended for it to be a ritualistic prayer simply read or recited over and over again at worship services, becoming almost zombie-like in its form. Quite the contrary, Jesus expected the Lord's Prayer to be an outline for how we connect to the Father and, thus, how we connect to one another.

Look at the dynamics of this amazing prayer. It begins with praise to God, and it's followed by us presenting our requests to him for his will to be done and also for our daily needs. We then pray for restoration in our relationships, and for the courage and wisdom to forgive. Finally, we pray for safety, protection, and strength to take on the temptations of the world and face down the Adversary.

When we pray the Lord's Prayer, we are not reciting a rote prayer experience; we are praying with a divine purpose. This is an outline, a map that ushers us into the presence of God and makes us one with God. This process does more than teach us to pray; it teaches us how to walk into God's presence and assimilate the awe.

How is your prayer life? The next time you say the Lord's Prayer, allow the words to rush over you, and soak them in. Then, say it again, and hear the voice of Jesus teaching his disciples, and understand that this way of praying would have seemed revolutionary to them. Finally, say it again and hear that this is just the beginning of our connection to God, the short form that focuses us on God's purpose for our lives. Following this guide not only will allow us to pray better but will actually draw us closer to God and to one another.

The Lord's Prayer must do that . . . Jesus just didn't *tell* us about this prayer; he *showed* it to us. That is how important it is.

DEEPEN

Find a quiet place to sit and study this Scripture passage, Matthew 6:5-13, which contains the words of the Lord's Prayer. Then, break the prayer into the parts whereby you see the purpose of each section (praise, requests, restoration, and so on). Why does the Lord's Prayer work better as an outline? Why does the prayer begin with words of praise for God? What is the importance of Jesus modeling the act of both asking for and granting forgiveness to others? Why does the Lord's Prayer place such importance on avoiding the temptations and snares of this world?

DEPLOY

Covenant to pray the Lord's Prayer as an outline for one week, praying it once a day. Keep a prayer journal, and write each day about your prayer experience, including the impact upon your attitude, your state of mind, and your feelings.

DISCERN

Pray: *Gracious God, thank you for the outline of the Lord's Prayer as a way for us to draw closer to you with our praise, concerns, joys, and requests. We appreciate that you just didn't "tell" us about how to pray but that you "showed" us and reiterated the importance of prayer. Open our hearts before you that we unveil ourselves openly to your grace. In Jesus' name. Amen.*

DAY FOURTEEN: UNFORCED RHYTHMS OF GRACE

Scripture: Read Matthew 11:28-30.

DISCOVER

SHANE: I mentioned in my book *A Positive Life* that in our house, you can't watch PG-rated movies until you have turned ten years old. It is a big milestone and one that is longed for and, when reached, much celebrated.

When our oldest daughter, Sarai Grace, turned ten, the first PG movie she wanted to see was *Star Wars*, which happens to be one of my favorites.

When I was younger than Sarai Grace, my grandfather took me to the local theater in the small town where we lived to see the premiere of George Lucas's new, exciting space drama. I remember watching half of the movie, wide-eyed and excited, and the other half with my head buried in my grandfather's shoulder, looking up only quickly enough to ask, "What happens next?" My grandfather, in his calm, caring tone, would always say, "You will just have to watch and see, sport." I thought, *That's the problem—I don't want to watch!* But I did, and it turned out fine.

By the time Sarai Grace and I sat down to watch *Star Wars*, I had prepared her for the vast cast of characters, including Darth Vader and all of the others who would be far more unnerving than anything she had seen before. She assured me that she was now big enough to handle the movie and that she was ready. I said OK and put the DVD in the player. We got settled on the sofa, complete with our popcorn and favorite soda. It was, for our family, one of those "historic" moments. I could almost hear drum rolls!

Within the first ten minutes, or somewhere around the first time we met Lord Vader, Sarai Grace, much like me years earlier, had buried her face into my shoulder. She looked up occasionally, when the silence would overtake the pounding music, and would ask, "What happens next, Daddy?" My response was always, "You will have to watch and see, sweetie." It was an almost perfect replay of what had happened nearly thirty years earlier in that small theater with my grandfather. Same movie, same setting, same questions.

It is not uncommon for children, of any age, size, or disposition, to ask that question: "What happens next?" It is also not uncommon for God's children to do the same thing. I know that I have reached a certain place in my life where I would love a blueprint for what comes around the corner next. However, my heavenly Father responds much as I did with Sarai Grace: "Watch and see."

The passage in Matthew 11 echoes Jesus' understanding of our fears, doubts, and uncertainties about the life we face. It is not easy to make that next turn, unsure of what will be waiting for us, or to jump into that breach, wondering what will catch us on the other side. But we turn and jump anyway, because Christ has called us to trust him and walk with him. His promise is that he will never put anything on us that is ill fitting or too heavy for us to handle. Quite the contrary, he will serenade our spirits with the "rhythms of grace" and make the journey with us.

Jesus' invitation is personal and powerful: "Keep company with me and you'll learn to live freely and lightly" (Matthew 11:30). In other words, you won't need to worry about what happens next because we have Jesus to guide the way. That sounds nice.

As we are searching for purpose in our lives, much of our struggle occurs when we forget that God walks with us. God's intention for our lives is simple—that we will be free from the lies that have bound our hearts for so long, that we may live boldly through his grace and rejoice. Beautiful! And it always applies, no matter what scene we may find ourselves facing.

DEEPEN

Reread Matthew 11:28-30 and watch for the following phrases (which may be different in your particular Bible translation):

"Come to me," "Get away with me," "Walk with me," "Watch how I do it," "Keep company with me." What do these phrases mean to you? What do they say about God's love and intentions in your life? Also, what does freedom mean to you? How would you define real freedom in your life? The opposite of *free* is *bound* or *captive*. In what ways are we bound by our lives—through sin? by our pasts? How does God make us free?

DEPLOY

Write a personal statement of "Spiritual Emancipation." What does it mean for us to be free from what the world has used to keep us in chains? How do we walk forward into that freedom? Make a list of ways in which you are held in bondage today, and reflect: how will you trust God to make you free?

DISCERN

Pray: *God of freedom, we are sorry for how much of our lives we live in bondage—bondage to sin, to our pasts, to our fears and doubts, to our mistakes, to our pride, to our ambitions. Gracious God, give us the freedom through Christ that transforms our hearts. Make us new in your grace, and then give us the strength to speak openly about that freedom so that others who are in bondage will find peace and contentment in you as well. Amen.*

DAY FIFTEEN: A GOD-REALITY

Scripture: Read Luke 12:25-34.

DISCOVER

The U.S. financial crisis of 2008 and 2009 shocked our nation. It was the worst financial climate since the Great Depression, and stalwart institutions in the economic community collapsed like startups in Silicon Valley had done a few years before. At the root of the problem was a series of issues that created a destabilization in the basic financial markets because of speculation, poor evaluation processes, and misguided values for properties and securities.

But even deeper, the crisis was just as personal in its nature as it was global. People were making risky purchases of properties they could not afford and certainly did not need. The result, when the market collapsed, was a rash of people who owned homes with complicated, expensive mortgages whose values had plummeted, leaving the owners and the mortgage companies or banks with depreciating assets covering much larger outstanding loans. People and institutions went bankrupt because of the scenario. In fact, every level of the economic structure of our nation was affected.

In the Gospel of Luke, Jesus would say the problem was rather simple. People had put their "treasure" into worthless or, at the least, volatile investments that could not in the end provide a return on their extended promise for prosperity. People had bet their businesses, homes, families, and lives on a "Get Rich Quick Reality" that could not be sustained. Eventually there would be a crash, and it was devastating. The economic world was left nearly spinning out of control.

Oddly enough, this is as much a spiritual problem as a financial one. At the heart of the issue is what we value in this world—what our primary objective really is. Jesus' answer to our situation is to recalibrate and trust a "God Reality" that puts a new set of ambitions and objectives at the center of our lives. Instead of money or possessions being the most valuable, this "God Reality" sets relationships and faith as the premium for wealth and success.

And best of all, a "God Reality" will meet *all* of our needs, not just our financial concerns. The full measure of our human experience—spiritual, relational and emotional—finds rest when we follow something that will not go bankrupt.

How many of us have invested our money in risky endeavors trying to find financial security? But how many of us have also invested our lives in risky circumstances, relationships, and patterns that lead to emotional and relational bankruptcy? We imagine the latter happens as much as the former. Jesus says to invest your life in Someone whose risk is minimal, but the return sure and secure. We cannot afford infinite losses. They mount up and will affect us. Trust in God's economy. It is never weak, undervalued, or close to collapse.

DEEPEN

In Luke 12:25-34, what is Jesus trying to teach us about trust? Why does it matter if we trust things of the world versus things of God? What happens when we put our trust in those finite makings of human beings? What happens when we trust a "God Reality" that is bigger, deeper, and sweeter than what the world can offer? Jesus says that we have provisions from God that will meet our needs. What do those provisions look like? How do they change and affect our lives?

DEPLOY

Create a "spiritual bankbook." What deposits have you made to your relationship with God lately? What withdrawals have you made? For what reasons have you made these withdrawals? Is your "spiritual balance" in the black or in the red? Explain why.

DISCERN

Pray: *Gracious God of all things, you have given us more than we deserve, and you offer us so much more through our relationship with Christ. Thank you for our many blessings and for the opportunity to go deeper in you. Lord, help us trust in your provisions for the whole of our lives, and not the earthly things that will eventually fade away. We love you. Amen.*

DAY SIXTEEN: OVERLOOKED AND IGNORED

Scripture: Read Matthew 25:31-40.

DISCOVER

If this passage teaches us anything, it is that God needs and uses our gifts to transform this world. We have often wished it were not so. It would be easier if God's plan did not rely on our gifts, which are so fickle and self-centered at times. But more than anything, we learn and are called to serve not only to make a difference in those whose lives we touch, but to be reminded of what such a life can mean for us. It is the extra mile, the next step in being more than a good "religious" person. It is the mark of a person captivated by God's love and wanting to share that love with others.

Jesus says that we stand on one side or the other of God's grace, when recognizing the work of God in the world. Matthew 25 says there is no gray area. Broken people need something foundational upon which we can build our lives and hopes. This isn't just a physical place, but something deeper, and it's one of the hardest things for those of us struggling with the displacement of chronic illness or chronic life situations to discover. We want our lives to matter, to mean something more than just getting by one day after another. As the passage insists, God expects that for us, too.

We want to belong to something or someone that the world cannot change. This feeling is the ache Adam and Eve felt when they were forced to leave the Garden, and each person has felt that same ache in various ways ever since. Something is missing. Something is not right. And deep down, we know it.

SHANE: I learned this firsthand from a friend named Tommy who literally arrived on our doorstep. He was thin, sickly, and obviously in distress. Tommy was crushed by regret and the consequences of bad decisions. That day he found himself standing on the doorstep of a stranger, a preacher nonetheless, desperate to believe in *anything*.

Tommy and I didn't have much in common beyond our common diagnoses of HIV. But over the year and a half that we met together to talk about life, we discovered another bond: our grandmothers. They had spoiled us. And Tommy remembered that his grandmother had loved him no matter what. Not many people in his life had done that. Our grandmothers had one other thing in common: they both had loved to sing "Jesus Loves Me" to us. Tommy's grandmother had passed away many years earlier, but he could still remember the sound of her voice and the way it gave him a sense of belonging and comfort.

One day I received a call: Tommy was in the hospital. By the time I arrived, he was slipping in and out of consciousness. When he realized where he was, he was unsettled and obviously distraught—his eyes were those of a man who was reacting as if something or someone was chasing him. He grew restless, and at one point the nurses were forced to restrain him. Nothing could calm him down. I began to talk to Tommy. He eased a bit, and I asked the nurses if I could remove his restraints. They agreed. By this time, everyone else had left his room, and I stood alone at the foot of his bed, thinking about the pain he felt and the real fear flooding over him in that moment. This was not just fear about his physical body, but also his fear of what came next.

I took the blanket and pulled the covers up around his wasted body. As my grandmother had done when I was a child, I tucked the blankets around Tommy and made sure that he was warm and snug. Then, as his grandmother had done, I leaned close to him, so close that our cheeks were touching, and I began to sing.

> Jesus loves me, this I know,
> for the Bible tells me so

Tommy's tension subsided; I felt his body relax and his eyes, so close to mine, close. I continued to sing.

> Little ones to him belong;
> they are weak, but he is strong.
> Yes, Jesus loves me!
> Yes, Jesus loves me!
> Yes, Jesus loves me!
> The Bible tells me so.

The room was silent. That little song, filled with such a huge promise, had brought him to somewhere he could stand as the waters rose around him. That simple song reminded him of the simple story he believed, even in the face of what was happening to him now.

Tommy died the next day, asleep in his hospital bed but standing, nonetheless, in his faith. He was on the right side of life, and he knew from where his strength came. What a homecoming that must have been! Now he was home, part of the family, where he belonged. He wasn't overlooked or ignored anymore. He wasn't hurting or feeling the sting of regret. And he wasn't alone.

Tommy's story reminds us that we are not alone either. No matter what the journey may feel like or what it may bring, the tears and struggle have purpose. The song holds true: "Jesus loves me"; the rest is just sweet melody.

DEEPEN

The story of the sheep and the goats in Matthew 25:31-40 shows us a picture of what happens when we miss meeting the needs of those around us. What do the ignored and the overlooked look like in your life? Why does this Scripture passage feel so personal? What does how we deal with those in need say about the rest of our spiritual walk?

DEPLOY

Write a letter as though you are a person who has been overlooked and ignored, and think about the following questions: What is it like to feel this way? Who do you blame? How do you feel about those who are supposed to love like Jesus but who have walked past you? In what way do you now connect to Jesus as one who had been forgotten and betrayed? Reflect upon the importance of why serving others changes our world.

DISCERN

Pray: *Gracious God, forgive us when we have passed by persons along the way who have been in need. Help us reach out and not only proclaim your love, but show your love by meeting others' needs and by standing alongside those who are marginalized, hurting, and forgotten. By taking the focus off our lives, we find our new, more complete purpose—the purpose you have for us. Amen.*

DAY SEVENTEEN: FULL APPETITES BUT HUNGRY SOULS

Scripture: Read Ecclesiastes 6:1-9.

DISCOVER

SHANE: I am not a very good cook, but my wife, Pokey, is. In fact, she learned very well from her grandmother, and I love almost 100 percent of whatever she makes. It helps that we have been together so long, because Pokey knows me well, and she knows my appetite.

But I am not finicky like some people I know. I like just about every type of food or dish I have tried. Each dish has its own qualities and flavors. Most of the time, I will try almost anything. That is not to say that I continue to eat everything I try, especially those foods that are bad for me. In fact, for many years I have watched my diet and made sure that I kept fat, sugar, carbs, and sodium to a minimum. I would put my diet up against anyone's, especially since mine is dictated by certain medicines or conditions whereby I need to follow as healthy a diet as possible. No, it is not the *type* of food I eat that is a problem; it is the *quantity*.

It doesn't matter if it is a banana split or rice cakes, I tend to eat too much of both. I learned several years ago that when we eat too much, the body actually rejects the amount of food and sends out a signal to the body to stop. But it also sends a signal that tells the body it can't assimilate the full measure of the nutrients and chemicals, leaving one feeling sluggish and down. This is why so many people collapse after Thanksgiving dinner. It is not just the chemicals in the turkey, but the excess of food that leaves a person dragging, even after a full meal.

The same is true for our spiritual lives. I know many people with full appetites and very hungry souls. They continue to feast on things of this world, gathering up material goods, relationships, or titles with the expectation that one or the other will make them whole. They don't. In fact, they are worse than before. It is a spiritual processed sugar—tasty going down, but an empty feeling when they finish. The soul rejects these items much like the body rejects the excess of food or hollow carbs. The result is a life that craves completeness and wholeness. I have seen it a hundred times: successful people come into my office, and they have the right cars, the right houses, the right friends, the right jobs; they go to the right vacation spots—but they just don't feel complete. They believe their lives are missing something. And they are.

In this passage of Scripture, the writer of Ecclesiastes says to take advantage of what God sends us *now*. Don't wait for something better to come along. It won't. What God sends is sufficient to feed our hungry souls and to supply our appetites. We will not leave unsatisfied. However, the real key to the passage is that it is up to us whether we will make this happen or not. We can starve to death on an inadequate diet, or even gorge ourselves on the right foods, but for the wrong reasons. The catch is to eat the right foods for the right reasons in the right manner. Don't take the buffet for granted, but also don't hog it or abuse it either. There is enough to go around, and it is meant to be shared. But it is also meant to fill us for the next day and the next part of the journey. We do not feast and then become spiritual couch potatoes. Quite the contrary, we feast in order to be fit and faithful.

In the future, watch your spiritual diet as much as your physical one. You might be surprised at what you have been living on—junk food for the heart and soul that pours empty calories into your life, leaving you hungry. God does more than fill you up; God provides the best of what our souls need to be healthy for the long term, which in turn changes everything else. Oh— and invite a friend. No meal should be enjoyed alone.

DEEPEN

Do you buy or consume things as a means for making yourself happy? Do you count on others, relationships, ambitions, or accolades to fill the empty places of your life? If so, what has been the result of that "diet"? How does it make you feel for the long haul? What would happen with a new diet of spiritual disciplines including prayer, fasting (from whatever keeps you from God), Bible study, and serving? Are you spiritually hungry? What keeps you from beginning this new diet immediately?

DEPLOY

Create a spiritual calorie journal. Just as you would record your caloric intake for the day, over the course of the next week make a list each day of things you do or things you experience that draw you away from God. Make a separate list of the items or experiences you have each day that draw you closer to God. What is the balance of the lists? Are you gaining spiritual muscle or fat?

DISCERN

Pray: *Gracious God of plenty, you have given the best of yourself to us in your Son, Jesus. He is sufficient for our full and empty places. Help us take him into our lives and learn more about his example, so that we might love and live like him in the world. We want to be spiritually healthy with good spiritual diets, Lord, but we have to start with the basics, the spiritual food groups that will make us so. Give us strength to pray, to study, to serve, and to worship. We know you will fill out the menu from there. Amen.*

DAY EIGHTEEN: WHAT ARE YOU REALLY LOOKING AT?

Scripture: Read Esther 5:9-13.

DISCOVER

The first time our friend attended the ministers' enrichment retreat, he was one year out of seminary. It was a great time of renewal and study, but it was also a special time to spend with friends in ministry. They were young pastors who had gone into ministry at roughly the same time and with similar life situations. They had young families, and all of them had ambitions for what they wanted to accomplish.

They were playfully competitive and pushed one another through the next task or opportunity. They knew that they would not all make the same decisions or have the same potential, but they supported and trusted one another. And they made a vow to be one another's biggest fans, no matter what successes or struggles they faced.

But the years moved on, and as this group of friends and colleagues saw their families grow and their careers lead in different directions, these pastor friends found it more and more difficult to spend time together. Eventually, some left the ministry or the pastorate altogether, while others faced a series of bad professional situations that led nowhere. And of course, there were others who experienced great blessings that led to incredible life chances. This, too, led to some distance between friends, as unfortunately happens.

Eventually, one of the friends acted out of frustration about how his life had turned out. He said something that was untrue about another friend and also very harmful to this friend's ministry. And to make matters worse, he continued to tell the same story over and over again, until his friend was forced to confront him. It was not an easy time. They had confided in each other over the years about deep personal issues, and now he was saying and doing things that were creating tension not only in their relationship but also harming someone's reputation.

When his friend confronted him, the young pastor was defensive and denied everything. But as more evidence was provided of how his words had been heard by so many and how they had created great distress, the pastor finally admitted that he had made the comments in question.

His friend asked him, "Why?" What had he done to make him so upset? The pastor who had made the untrue comments responded, "I am jealous of the success you have had." His reply stunned his friend. They had agreed to support each other no matter what, but the young pastor was expressing a very human emotion, and, as these emotions often do, it revealed a very ugly side of humanity.

The friends left their conversation clearly at odds, both hurt by the situation. One was embarrassed; the other hurt and mistrustful. They not only let their emotions get the better of them, but they allowed their humanity to dictate how they left their relationship.

For several months, the friends did not speak. Neither felt the need or the desire to go down that road. And so they retreated into their feelings and allowed their friendship to suffer.

Finally, the wife of one of them encouraged her husband to call the other. "I don't really want to," was his reply. "Besides, he is the one who should call me." His wife, who is much wiser in these situations than he is (we all agree!), said, "*Should's* and *ought's* matter very little in these situations. Someone has to act like Jesus." Her words hurt, but her husband knew they were true.

He put aside his pride and called his friend. At first he was resistant to talk, but then they agreed to meet. After several awkward moments, he finally said, "I'm glad you called. I have been meaning to do it myself, but I just . . . couldn't." For some reason, it didn't matter whether he believed his friend or agreed with him. The friend who made the call kept hearing his wife's words, "Someone has to act like Jesus."

"Acting like Jesus" is not always easy or fun. It requires a sacrifice from us, a change in our perceptions, and a putting aside of our pride to be able to meet and see people as Jesus did. But it is also the only way to repair the breaches of our relationships.

When these friends met to talk, it was tough, but over the course of the conversation they found the beginning of their friendship again. They laughed. They cried. And they talked honestly about other things in their lives that had led them to focus pride and frustration on each other. In the end, they prayed for each other. And even today, they are still working back into a trustful relationship, but God has been good, and they are healing.

So many times in our lives, we look at the wrong things or at things other than what God intends for us to look at, because we are afraid of focusing our lives on the most important things. We strain not to make eye contact with those who love us best or who tell us the truth, and instead of growing closer to Christ, we drift away from him and from one another.

But as our friend's wife said, we are not called to wallow in our self-pity and hurt but to "respond like Jesus." It is the only way to recover our relationships and to put down the bitterness that so often holds us hostage. God does not care about who is "right" and who is "wrong"; he cares about who is acting like him and who is serving as a witness for what reconciliation really looks like.

DEEPEN

The Scripture passage in Esther 5:9-13 is about pride. Haman wants people to notice him. When Mordecai doesn't, Haman is hurt and offended. Have you ever been offended by the way someone has treated you? Have you had your feelings hurt because of something someone has said or done? Have you allowed those feelings to preoccupy you and to consume you? How does that affect the rest of your life? What do you believe "acting like

Jesus" looks like? How would being preoccupied with a lifestyle that follows the example of Jesus change our current situations and relationships?

DEPLOY

Make of list of your "preoccupations." How do they dominate your life? Now, make a list of specific ways you can change your focus. What does that list look like? What effect would making these changes have on your life? Take action to implement these changes. For example, call a person who has hurt you, and offer forgiveness and the chance for restoration. Change your view, and watch what God will do.

DISCERN

Pray: *God of second chances, thank you for not looking at us through the eyes of our broken lives, but through the eyes of Jesus. We love your grace and your unconditional connection to us. Help us share that with others and to work at restoring our relationships. Give us the courage to face our fears, our doubts, and our broken edges and to trust that even in the worst of situations, you are a God who puts us back together. Amen.*

DAY NINETEEN: FROM RATIONS TO PASSIONS

Scripture: Read Nehemiah 13:7-13.

DISCOVER

DEANNA: Over the years of being an NFL wife, I have watched year after year the incredible amount of work that goes into getting ready for the season. Many people view the NFL as a glamorous lifestyle, and in many ways, it is. But 99 percent of the work that goes on behind the scenes is like any other job. It requires people putting in very long hours studying, training, and preparing themselves not only to give their individual best, but also to work together as a team.

One very important time during the season is the preseason. Many consider the preseason games to be unimportant. But they are critical for getting a true perspective for how the team might perform during the regular season. Coaches use this time for assessing how well the newer players assimilate into the organization's game plan. And it is also a time for the young guys to earn their slots by showing the coaches what they can do. Preseason is an opportunity to show your passion for playing the game and to make an impression.

At other times in the months leading up to the regular season, coaches are looking for different things. Spring offers a time to form the team according to basic talents, skills, and needs. Summer involves more specific preparation as the team roster and the depth chart take shape. But by the time preseason begins, it is about heart. It is about whether that twenty-two-year-old kid has the soul to play, game in and game out, and to give his all.

Many people watching at home might never realize the importance of these games. The franchise players and veterans who are assured of their positions play very little. But next time you watch a preseason game, watch closely *the guys who are on the field*. Watch their intensity and their level of excitement. The coaches are watching. And by watching these qualities, you will be able, almost to a tee, to size up what the team will look like once the first regular season game is played. Of course, once the season is under way, each player's passion for the game must continue, not so much to earn a playing spot, but to earn the win.

Isn't it funny how God's plan for us is like a season in the NFL? We are called to share our gifts for God's greater purpose. Then, our level of passion for God's plan determines how much of ourselves we put "on the field" and how much we trust that God is doing something special. But it doesn't stop there. Our passion for Christ then walks us through the ups and downs of life and is, in so many instances, the difference between getting by and prevailing.

Nehemiah was distressed with his people because they had lost their passion. They had gone to living off the reserves and rations of their emotions and their skills. He wanted more from them, not because he was some unreasonable taskmaster, but because he knew they had it in them. Their passion showed him what God could do through them. Nehemiah knew that the level of their passion could be a "game changer."

God wants us to be "game changers" by living passionately for him. We were not meant to live on the rations but to feast on the joy, excitement, and speed of the life in front of us. Don't limp by—run, and become all that God has in store. God is watching, cheering us on, knowing that we have so much more inside of us.

DEEPEN

What is your passion level for Christ? Do you "get by on the rations" or live in the passion for the moment? What qualities show God that we are "on fire" for what he has given for us to be and do? What keeps us from living out those qualities? What can we learn from Nehemiah's encouragement of his people for making the most of what God has intended for us?

DEPLOY

Write down your current schedule, accounting for all of your time and activities. How do your lifestyle and your schedule reflect your current passion level? Go through each item on your schedule and discuss how much it contributes to God's plan each day. In what ways do the "normal" things of life provide for a closer walk with God? Finally, what new thing is God calling you to do and live out in order to live up to your potential?

DISCERN

Pray: *Gracious God, thank you for passionately loving us. You have given the best of yourself to us in Jesus. You did not withhold even your own Son. Sometimes we take that for granted. Help us treasure Jesus and what he has done for us. Give us joy to celebrate and to live passionately so that others will see you through us. Amen.*

DAY TWENTY: WISDOM AT HOME

Scripture: Read Proverbs 14:2-13.

DISCOVER

SHANE: A friend of mine called me to say that he and his wife were getting a divorce. It was a shock to everyone. They were one of those couples whom people thought would be together forever. Jim and Sally had been high-school sweethearts and had loved each other as long as we had known them. They appeared to be the perfect match.

But over the years Jim's job took him away from home often. He was always an overachiever, and he was determined, since he came from very modest surroundings, to make a life for Sally and himself that was much more than they had known growing up.

Sally was a schoolteacher, almost the perfect example of how you might picture a dedicated schoolteacher. She was sweet and beautiful with a bubbly personality. People could not help liking her.

At first their life together went as planned. Jim continued to do better and better in his company, and Sally enjoyed her teaching position. They had a daughter, Sylvia, six years after getting married, quickly followed by a son, little Jim.

That is when the cracks in their relationship began to form. Sally needed and wanted Jim to be home more. But Jim was at a stage where his job required him to be away more often than not. The breach between their wants and expectations continued to grow, and their relationship deteriorated.

Soon, Sally found herself the object of the affections of the father of one of her students. This man said to her the sorts of things that Jim had once said to her, and they made her feel beautiful and wanted. She would organize meetings with parents just to see the father of the student, and she even became friends with the man's wife. Eventually, instead of going home, Sally began going out for drinks after work, meeting other teachers, parents, and this gentleman in particular. The relationship became physical one night when Sally least expected it. She had been drinking that evening and had let her guard down. The verbal affections and compliments became one touch, and then another, until they found themselves at a cheap hotel, giving over their marriage covenants for a few moments of pleasure.

A few weeks before, when other friends had warned Sally that she was playing with fire, she told them that it all was harmless and that she could handle it, and that she felt she deserved to have a few moments of fun. But she couldn't handle what was happening, and then the flames eventually burned her.

The saddest part about this story and those like them is that no one I have met woke up one day and decided to ruin his or her life. Quite the contrary, these people fretted for weeks over how their lives were moving until, bit by bit, they found their defenses down just a little farther one day than they had been the day before. The fall was simple but devastating.

My wife and I have talked about similar times in our marriage when I worked so hard at being a good Christian pastor that I forgot to be the husband and father that God intended. My wife found herself further and further from my heart until one day she stumbled along the path. It was so difficult for us, but so much *both* our faults. We had seen the warning signs. We knew it was coming.

The writer of Proverbs 14 warns the reader that foolish living is bad. Foolish living, without watching the signs all around you, is destructive. Everything can appear to be together, but as the Scripture states, "when the laughter ends, the grief remains" (verse 13).

God has more in store for us. One of the struggles of the chronic life is that we allow the aches and pain to convince us that we deserve certain negative turns and twists. Or at the least, we mistakenly feel that we can handle what comes our way. But nothing could be farther from the truth. Our fragile nature must always watch for what is around the corner. Unexamined friendships can become dangerous, our actions can become devastating, and the consequences so hard to repair.

God plans and expects a rich life for us. It is not God who walks away from the path. I read this proverb when my own life was coming apart, and I wished someone had pointed it out to me sooner. I had been one of those friends who had encouraged Sally to slow down and to look at what was happening. I even sent her this scripture to read. But she chose a different path.

We cannot become all that God has in store for us if we fail to connect to people of character and integrity. We must live with wisdom as our guide. Wisdom cannot be bought in a store. It is not won at a fair. Wisdom and reason do not drop from the sky. They begin at home, and the mass of them, or lack thereof, leads our path from there.

DEEPEN

What does the writer of Proverbs try to teach us about life in this passage? Why are the qualities of a moral life so important to watch for and to consider? What are the ramifications of a life that ignores these principles? How do we fail God and each other when we allow foolish things to dominate our lives? Is the writer of Proverbs talking to you? If so, what in your life needs adjustment before it is too late?

DEPLOY

OK, some truth time. Take a blank piece of paper and write down the one thing that is most harmful to your life; is it a name? a relationship? an ambition? an addiction? What can and should you do to address this strug-gle in your life? Now, whom will you tell and confide in, in order to find help in addressing the problem? The writer of Proverbs says we do not deal with these situations alone. Who will be your eyes and ears, mindful of how your life is proceeding?

DISCERN

Pray: *Gracious God, we are sorry for how we have failed you and one another. We have tried to be our own gods, assuring ourselves that we can handle whatever comes our way. But we were wrong: we are not enough. We need you. Give us wisdom to seek you and trust you. Give us strength to follow where you lead. And give us grace that we might begin today. We love you. Amen.*

CHAPTER FIVE

THE CURE: RESPONSE

D EANNA: It still amazes me what a powerful impact a person's last name can have on raising awareness for an event or even raising funds for a particular cause. Of course, it wasn't always like that for our family. For most of my life, I lived in a working-class family with hard-working parents. My childhood was extremely common in one sense, though I had loving parents and the kind of close-knit family that is the greatest blessing of anyone's life.

When I met Brett Favre, I did not expect much to change. I fell in love with the legendary Number Four long before anyone realized that he would become one of the greatest quarterbacks (and yes, I am prejudiced about that!) in NFL history. In fact, Brett received the last available scholarship at the University of Southern Mississippi, as a defensive back. He was eventually made the seventh-string quarterback after the coach saw him throwing the football with a teammate. Later, in a regular season game against Tulane, the coach at the time, Jim Carmody, finally played this unheralded quarterback from Kiln, Mississippi. The rest, as they say, is history.

Over the years, our journey has taken us from the quiet town of Hattiesburg, Mississippi, where Brett became a local star, to Atlanta, to Green Bay, where he became part of a legendary environment of sports heroes that includes the great Coach Vince Lombardi and players such as Bart Starr and Paul Hornung. Later Brett's career would lead us to New York and then to Minnesota.

Along the way, Brett and I had our share of ups and downs. Many people know that our fairy tale had a few "villains," including Brett's addiction to painkillers and alcohol, and the tragic, sudden deaths of Brett's father and my brother, Casey. But our time in each place we have lived has also been magical in so many ways, and we've had the opportunity to participate in helping each community of which we've been a part. It was part of our routine to attend social functions, banquets, fundraisers, and more in an effort to help charities carry on their good work. And of course, we were also connected to our local parishes in both Hattiesburg and Green Bay and did what good Roman Catholics do in terms of sharing God's blessings.

But it wasn't until my bout with breast cancer that God truly showed me the importance of really responding to the needs of others. And it was during this revelation that I learned that "response" is a scriptural method or tool that God uses to move you through your own struggles and to redefine your priorities and life.

It was a rather ordinary day when the doctor called to tell me that the lump we had discovered was indeed cancer. This started a long period of treatment and recuperation that ultimately changed our family's life. The profoundness of any such event on a person and those around them is significant. But for me, it also changed the way I saw the world. I had always had extended family around me whenever trouble or struggle occurred in my life. As I mentioned, I come from a tight-knit family. But my bout with cancer showed me that not everyone has either the connection of family or the resources needed for the most basic of tasks and routines. The more time I spent at treatment and trying to fight my own battle with cancer, the more God showed me those around me who did not have it so easy.

These revelations and relationships haunted me. I couldn't imagine a life without a supportive husband, mother, sister, or family who were there by my side. Thus, I woke up every day with two things on my mind—trying to get well, and thinking about the person I had met at the clinic the previous day who didn't have even a small portion of what I had to win the battle.

"I felt the need to do something . . . anything," my coauthor, Shane, says in one of his previous books, *You Can't Do Everything . . . So Do Something*. I didn't know Shane during this time of my life, but I understood that spirit nonetheless. I wanted to do everything, but I quickly realized that even with all of the blessings our family had, we did not have enough to do all that we encountered. But we could do *something*.

That is when I created the Favre 4 Hope Foundation. The purpose of the foundation is to provide resources in terms of basic assistance for women who are undergoing treatment for breast cancer. We are not raising money for research or for treatment; we know there are other agencies for both. The purpose of our foundation is to help young women, wives, and mothers have enough money to make ends meet while undergoing treatment.

Some people have questioned the simplicity of the foundation's purpose, and I have even had people ask why I don't spend more time on other pursuits. But this is what God has called me to do in response. This is my *something*. I have heard Shane talk about how his heart was changed when he realized the plight of those living with HIV in developing countries who did not have the blessings of resources and family that he had. Even with his own journey so closely tied to the subject, those stories of need around the world had a significant impact upon him and led to the creation of his Maji Project for providing rehydration kits for those in need. This project is not going to meet every need. But to the people it assists, don't tell them that it does not make a difference.

I feel the same way about our foundation. It is our way to do *something*, to respond. And it is about more than just making us feel better or providing charity. This work is a spiritual activity. There is a biblical imperative to its mission. In Mark 1, a man with leprosy sat by the city gate day after day, waiting for someone to come by. Finally, he heard about Jesus, a teacher and rabbi who could do great things and heal people. As Jesus drew closer, the man called out to him, "If you want to, you can make me well again" (Mark 1:40). I have always thought this was an odd way to approach Jesus. But do you know the rest of that story? Jesus reached out his hand, touched the man, and healed him (see Mark 1:41-42). We know that Jesus was always willing to be involved in people's lives, and we know that Jesus made an incredible difference in so many different ways.

But if you read the story again, you get the picture. This man with leprosy does not know Jesus. However, he believes that the stories he has heard about this man from Nazareth are true. There were lots of people who had passed by this man, and who had the power to make some kind of difference in his life, but they didn't act. Why? They chose not to do so. They did not have the "will."

I love how the Scripture reads from this point. It says that Jesus was "Moved with pity," and said "I want to" and "Be healed!" (verse 41). Jesus crossed the line. He went from having *the ability* to do something to actually *doing* it. In one moment, Jesus transformed religion. All the rabbis who had walked by before and even the people who had shouted a prayer or a promise to pray hadn't gone this far. Jesus went beyond merely *understanding*, and even beyond *compassion*; he *responded* to the man's need. This wasn't about Jesus, the disciples, the religious leaders, or even the crowd. For probably the first time in this man's life, Jesus made the story about *him*. Jesus' response not only healed the man's body; it gave him an identity, healed his heart, and changed his life.

All of us are called to respond to whatever God is doing in our lives. True, most of us will not be able to use our names alone to hold fundraisers or add to the validity of a cause, and those who are able to do so in glory to God should feel truly humbled and blessed. But all of us, the Bible says, have been gifted with *something*, and our only responsibility is to *respond*. And yet, in that response we go from being a spectator in the world, engaged only by our own situation, to diving into the lives of others and making a difference. And did I mention that the real transformation appears in us, too, and not just in those whom we help!

Over the next ten days, we encourage you to *respond*. It is time for us to make this story interactive, to get out of our comfort zones and become "the hands and feet of Jesus." We are no longer simply trying to get our minds around the situation or our hearts around the circumstances. It is time to get our hands around the solution and make something happen.

SHANE: I have a therapist friend who asks her clients, as part of their counseling, to volunteer doing some work for persons who are under-resourced. When I asked my friend why she did this, she said that most people's problems begin with only thinking about themselves. When we get our hands into the muck of someone else's life and work at making a difference, we pull back the veil of our own situation, and real healing can begin. I know this focus firsthand. One day, I was suffering from my own illnesses, and the next day I was a fellow soldier in the battle who also happened to be ill. My friends, there was a huge difference.

Quite simply, we are praying that God will wreak havoc on you in the next ten days—in a good way, of course! We want God to amaze you as he pushes you out of your comfort zone and into that *something* through which you were born to serve. It will not be easy; I'll admit it is hard to shake the mind-set that life is really just about us. But in the end, stripping away this understanding of life is the most healing, life-giving thing we can do. And it will certainly rip us away from our bent to chronic patterns and lives.

So, yes, we are hoping that you will get a little uncomfortable, that God will show up in a mighty way, and that ten days from now, after you have worked through this part of the spiritual treatment plan, the Holy Spirit will have "spun you around" a couple of times, sending you to respond to the needs of the world. In essence, we hope you are not the same.

Let's pray:

Gracious God, we all have a part to play, and you have crafted a special place and purpose for each of us. Give us your heart to connect in that something that you have so delicately, lovingly, and powerfully put together for us. We want to be amazed as we live into "the hands and feet" of your Son. God, we pray that you will pierce our hearts and open our souls to you. Help us give away our selfishness and embrace a new approach and a new appraisal of what you are doing. We want to change the world—at least our little part of it. As the popular hymn says, dear Lord, "let it begin with me." Amen.

RECOMMENDED RESOURCES

Sjogren, Steve. *Conspiracy of Kindness*, revised and updated ed. Ventura, Calif.: Regal Books, 2008.

Sjogren, Steve. *101 Ways to Reach Your Community*. Colorado Springs, Colo.: NavPress, 2000.

TEN-DAY SPIRITUAL TREATMENT PLAN FOR RESPONSE

DAY TWENTY-ONE: LOOKING FOR THE LIVING AMONG THE DEAD

Scripture: Read John 11:1-44.

DISCOVER

SHANE: Tombs come in all shapes and sizes. How many times have you watched a person's life self-destruct while you wondered why that person couldn't see the problem or make a different choice? How many times have we found ourselves a second too late or an inch too short to take hold of something better? Do you live with any regrets? We all do. Do you have any relationships you wish you could "do over" or take one more moment with? Do you have any words or mistakes that you wish you could turn back the hand of time and make right? Have you left anything undone because of doubt or fear or confusion, something you wish you had one more chance to face? Again, we all do.

There were four different reactions to Lazarus's situation as described in John 11:1-44—the reactions of the disciples, of Martha, of Mary, and of the crowd. These different reactions tell us much about the characters involved but, when we pay attention, even more about ourselves.

We can see ourselves in these characters because death and mourning, of various kinds, are the great equalizers of life. Invariably, during such times our true strengths and weaknesses emerge. Death knows no socioeconomic status, no nationality, no religion, no political persuasion, no life well lived or bad choices made, no criminal or saint. The story of Lazarus is really the story of how any of us react when death and grief and trouble come a-knockin'; that is the reason for Jesus' tears. Jesus didn't weep for the deceased Lazarus; Lazarus was in better shape than any of the others. Jesus wept for the mourners who were weeping without really knowing why. He wept for the disciples whose fears, once again, had gotten the best of them. He wept for Thomas, who had all the courage he needed but none of the hope he so desperately wanted. He wept for Martha, who could give the right answers but couldn't ask honest questions. And Jesus wept for Mary, who believed that God had vanished. But, friends, here is the beauty and also the burden of this passage: Jesus wept, too, for you and me, and for every lonely tomb before which we will ever stand.

That day at Lazarus's tomb, there were so many dead. Jesus stood in the midst of friends and strangers and followers and wondered why they couldn't see what he saw. "My disciples, you don't have to be afraid; I am not afraid. Thomas, you don't have to be a martyr—all you have to do is trust and follow and be amazed! Martha, don't you understand what I am saying? I'm not just fulfilling a religious objective—I'm talking about real life that lasts forever and makes this life look like a momentary displeasure. Mary . . . sweet Mary . . . don't give up! You sat at my feet for a reason. You knew that God was close that day. He is close now, even if you can't seem to find him." Jesus stood there and looked from one to another, grieving all of that death and wondering why it would continue to be so difficult for them and for us to see something better. Jesus wept for what they had done and had not done, for where they had been and for where they had refused to go. He wept for how the world had made them cynical, fearful, hopeless, confused, and sad. At some point, the lump in his throat began to hurt and the hole in his heart began to throb, and it was too much. . . . He stood at the tomb, and the God of the universe wept. He wept because those he loved were living like they were already dead.

We are to live. Live boldly, surely, certainly, faithfully. We live as those who have been raised from the dead. We live to make a difference, to respond to the needs of the world, and to become all that God needs us to be.

DEEPEN

Read John 11:1-44 again. Which of the four reactions to Lazarus's situation best describes yours—that of the disciples, Mary, Martha, or the crowd? How does your reaction decide the depth of your experience of God's miracle? Who saw the blessing of Lazarus's resurrection most clearly that day, and why? Describe what you think Jesus' tears were about; what would upset Jesus enough that he wept at the tomb of Lazarus, though he had raised people from death before?

DEPLOY

What are the principal characteristics of Mary, Martha, the disciples, and the crowd? What persons do you know who fit into each of these categories? How do these persons affect you and your decisions during the day? What should you do to either change this relationship or deepen it in order to have a more healthy expression of what God is teaching us at the tombs of our lives?

DISCERN

Pray: *God of life and death, you bring us to the tombs of our lives—including those "tombs" that are emotional, intellectual, relational, and spiritual in nature—and you show us the way to live beyond their captivity. God, walk us away from those tombs. Help us find places of life, and set these as the example of who we are in you. Amen.*

DAY TWENTY-TWO: DO YOU REALLY WANT TO GET WELL?

Scripture: Read John 5:1-9.

DISCOVER

DEANNA: I remember days during my treatment for cancer when I couldn't decide if I wanted to be well or not. I hurt too badly. The nausea was too great, the aches too painful. I felt so bad that I couldn't decide if it was worth the effort and the fight to get well.

Certainly, I don't know what it is like to sit by the healing pool at Bethsaida all day for years, waiting for someone to push me into the waters when they are stirred, but I can imagine that you grow weary as much from the waiting as from the disease itself.

Living the chronic life is somewhat like the experience of the man by the pool in John 5. Each day, we wait for the next shoe to drop. We may wake up feeling so much better, only to have it wear us down by the end, and we find that we are back where we started. Chronic relationships and marriages and work situations are like this, too. We believe that progress is just around the corner, only to have a too-human situation take place that pushes us back into our doubts and mistrust.

Jesus' question of the man by the pool was telling: "Do you want to get well?" In other words, he was asking, "After all you have been through, after sitting at this pool for all of these years, after *this* being all you have known, are you sure you want this to change? Are you prepared for what this change will mean in your life?" It sounds like a silly question to ask of someone who had been waiting at the pool for so long, but it makes perfect sense. There comes a point in our battle where the question is not whether we can be healed or whether God can work in our lives, but the real question is whether we are *willing* for it to happen. Jesus pushes us out of our comfort zones and asks, "Are you really ready to trust me?"

"Yes," was the man's answer. Jesus could tell that he meant it. On the spot, the man was made well. Not only was his body changed, but his life was changed as well. Healing didn't just mean a new physical state; it also meant the chance to move out of this neighborhood of broken lives into a new place where one could make a difference.

What about you? Maybe you have been living in this condition of the chronic life for so long, you wonder if you can live any other way. Now God is offering you something different. But it will take moving from the poolside, where you have learned to cope, and trusting that God can give you a new chance for new relationships and a new future. It will take more than just courage; it will also take a deep-seated willingness and the belief that having your life change is all that really matters.

My prayer for you, as it is for all of us, is that we might watch the waters stir inside each of us and that we will follow where Christ leads. It won't be easy, but it will certainly be for our good, and the result is that we will never be the same.

DEEPEN

Reread John 5:1-9, and reflect on this question: Are you really ready to be healed? Or have you become content with living in a chronic state of life? What happens when you voice your willingness to be healed? What changes can you expect from this new life? What do you think happened to the man at the pool in John 5 on the *next* day of his life? Do you believe God abandoned him? If not, how do you believe God would have continued to work in this man's life to bring renewal and restoration?

DEPLOY

What keeps you from asking for God to heal the whole of your life? What does real healing mean for you? Make a list of what keeps you "by the pool" and from being healed. What do you need to "set down" in your life in order to respond to God's urging to be healed and begin again?

DISCERN

Pray: *Gracious God of healing, we know that not all healing is physical or miraculous in its effect. Some healing is about relationships being put back together and mind-sets being changed. Keep us focused on you, Lord, that we might see how you are moving all around us. We want to be changed and grow, so that we can become witnesses for your grace to others. We need you to make us whole. Amen.*

DAY TWENTY-THREE: READY TO SERVE AT A MOMENT'S NOTICE

Scripture: Read John 12:20-26.

DISCOVER

SHANE: My wife and I have heard the cry that parents dread to hear. It is that cry of pain that tells you your child is hurt or sick. We can be in a deep sleep and not hear thunder, but let one of our children begin to cry or whimper because of a high fever or some other illness and we will hear it as though they are next to us. Or we can be in the middle of a large crowd along with other people and their children, and still we can hear the specific cry of our child clearly. It is God's great instinctual gift to parents that we will not miss the cry of the ones we love the most when they are in need.

In the same way, children also know their parents' voices just as clearly. My children have said they have been on the other side of a store and have heard us call. Or my wife will call out the back door of our house to announce it is time for dinner, and our children will come running. We know the voice, we know the intentions of the cry or the call, and we respond.

God is no different. His voice, the Scripture tells us, is like that of a shepherd whose sheep know his voice clearly. But we have to listen. When we do not listen, we wander and stray and find ourselves in difficult places.

The chronic life grows so difficult because the voices we follow do not have our best interest at heart. We follow the same unhealthy patterns time and time again, only to find ourselves in the same situations as we try to make sense of why the path has landed us here once more. *If only we had listened to the right voice.*

The Scripture says that God's voice is unmistakable and that its purpose is to provide guidance for our lives. It calls us to follow where God leads. And God's voice is not a faint voice. Sure, we can become masters at ignoring it, but always know it is there. The Scripture says that God's voice points us to a better direction, to a better path, or to a better blessing. But for so many of us, we simply walk the other way.

Let us ask this question: How much does God love you? Better yet, how much do you love your own children? your spouse? your friends? No matter how much we love those who are most dear to us, God loves us even more. It is hard to fathom, but the Scripture says that God's love is greater than anything we can know. So, why would we not want to hear that voice, to follow God's guidance?

When we hear the voice of God, we find our life. When we hear God's voice, we see the world more clearly. When we hear God's voice, we see our brothers and sisters differently. When we hear God's voice, we understand. When we hear the voice of God, we set our paths straight. When we hear the voice of God, we discover our strength for tomorrow. When we hear the voice of God, we watch him make something of the pain and the potential. Listen, then! God has something to say to us. Hear that voice! Don't miss those words.

DEEPEN

In Romans 12:2, Paul says to focus yourself on God and he will change you "from the inside out." What does that mean? What does it mean to be conformed to the world as opposed to transformed through God's grace? What does a transformed life look like? What does it sound like to hear the voice of God? What does God's voice offer when we drop everything and follow him?

DEPLOY

Write down thoughts about what you believe Jesus means when he talks about "burying a grain of wheat" and "harvesting new life." What does it mean to put aside old burdens and hurts and to begin again? What does that picture look like? What keeps us from listening to those calls in our lives? Why is that process so painful for us?

If you are regularly keeping a journal as you work through this spiritual treatment plan, by now your journal may be filling up with lists and procedures that are showing you a consistent message: the more we follow after Christ, the more we find the true direction and destination for our lives. How is that message shaping up in your life? What mid-course corrections are needed?

DISCERN

Pray: *Gracious God, help us follow where you lead. So many times we tend to go off on our own paths, and we find ourselves lost and unaware of where to go next. Give us wisdom to hear your voice and to follow where you lead. Then, help us mark the way for others by our lives, our example, and our actions. Amen.*

DAY TWENTY-FOUR: HE COULDN'T WAIT UNTIL MORNING!

Scripture: Read Acts 16:25-34.

DISCOVER

SHANE: My wife, Pokey, and I recently attended a gathering of senior pastors and spouses of the hundred largest United Methodist churches in the United States (as determined according to average weekly worship attendance). The meeting was informative, challenging, and reassuring as we met new friends and shared with older ones.

One of our responsibilities at this gathering was to discuss how the hundred largest congregations can assist the denomination as a whole in the century's new reality of ministry. Some of the statistics and the conversation we shared about the rapidly declining numbers in worship attendance and church membership today were difficult to assimilate. But as sobering as the data may be, the opportunities for how the local church remains the "hope of the world" are even more significant.

John Wesley, the founder of Methodism, faced a similar crisis in his own denomination, the Church of England. Wesley would look out and see the empty churches, but even more important, he saw the empty spirits, and he decided that something must be done. And the "something" began with *him*—with his own mind-set and thinking. He took to heart several of the apostle Paul's sermons where he said that we must become what God needs us to be by first "renewing" our minds. In Wesley's day, that was more than an intellectual exercise; it also symbolized the "way we saw the world, God, and God in the world."

And no matter his personal feelings about the new places God was sending him, John Wesley left the comfort of his local church and traveled 250,000 miles to preach 40,000 sermons in the countryside. He did this because the people were there and God needed him to go. Even though he detested both travel and open-air preaching, he did them because that is what God called him to do.

Wesley realized that, as the Scripture tells us, in giving our lives away in service to Christ we find real life, and it makes all the difference. He certainly would have preferred to have stayed in the safety of his local pulpit, but we are so glad he didn't. His message of hope, a new beginning, and a God who yearns to be in our lives profoundly changed the face of Christianity for generations to come. Like Paul and Silas in the story in Acts 16, John Wesley *couldn't wait* until morning to make a difference. He had to go "now" because God's plan required it of him.

And Jesus hopes that we won't be able to wait until morning to make a difference, either. No matter where God is calling you, you can be assured of a couple of things. First, God has gone before you and prepared your path. And second, if we will let him, God will transform our words, our intentions, and our thinking to mirror his heart. People not only will see this difference; they will find an open door to so much more.

DEEPEN

Read Acts 16:25-34 again. Why do you think the jailer was so affected by Paul's and Silas's behavior? Why would the jailer have any context for knowing what it means to "put [his] entire trust in the Master Jesus" (verse 31 *The Message*); where would he have learned these things? Discuss the scene of the jailer immediately taking Paul and Silas to see his family. How do you think the family responded? What would it have been like to see "the entire family" put their trust in God? Why is it so important to foster a good example in Christ, as Paul and Silas did?

DEPLOY

Make a "rejoice list"—a list of those areas where you need to celebrate more. What keeps people from making such lists? Now, make a list of family people in your life who need to draw closer to God. What can you do to show them God's love and grace?

DISCERN

Pray: *Gracious God of wholeness, you call us from the prisons of bad attitudes, bad relationships, and bad decisions to believe and trust that you are working something special in our lives. Help us put down the chains that bind us and not only receive the grace you offer, but share and model that grace for others. We love you. Amen.*

DAY TWENTY-FIVE: *NOTHING* MEANS "NOTHING"

Scripture: Read Romans 8:31-39.

DISCOVER

Recently the United States Navy released information on a newly built warship that was launched from a naval construction area in Mobile, Alabama. This new warship is supposed to be the toughest, fastest warship of its class by far. The pictures and video from its inaugural voyage touring the Gulf of Mexico were impressive. It has a cruising speed many knots faster than the next fastest warship. And with its hull of steel covering over 90 percent of the craft, it is incredibly tough and also quite menacing-looking.

The first news conference about this warship was filled with proclamations of what the ship could do. When discussing the ability to outrun hostile vessels, the commander mentioned that the ship had both the capacity to outrun any other vessel and the firepower to stand and fight if necessary. It was said that no type of conventional weapon or missile is strong enough to compromise the hull of this craft. At the news conference, the commander repeated this assertion over and over again, until finally a reporter asked about nonconventional missile systems such as nuclear. The commander was forced to "re-qualify his words" so that "nothing" meant "within a certain category." In other words, *nothing* really *did not* mean "nothing"; it meant nothing "normal." The captain finished the interview by saying, "There is always 'something' that can harm any vessel. No vessel is impervious to every attack or weapon."

So, then, when does *nothing* really mean "nothing," and when does *nothing* mean "most things"? It is a good question, not just in terms of impressive new warships, but for our spiritual walk as well.

In Romans 8 the apostle Paul says that "nothing . . . absolutely nothing" can separate us from God's love in Christ Jesus. He repeats this claim by giving examples of what these "nothings" are, including death, angels, demons, principalities, and so on. For Paul, *nothing* means "nothing." With human-made items like warships, there is always a limit. They are finite, human-made, and thus can be destroyed, no matter how indestructible we may believe them to be. Remember the *Titanic*?

But in God's economy *nothing* means "nothing." Period. Life will do its best to convince us otherwise; to make us question whether God can keep God's promise. But the Scripture is absolutely clear. God's love is beyond even the most ardent attacks of the Adversary—spiritually speaking, attacks both "conventional" and "nuclear." Though we may feel pressed and worried, the hull of God's grace cannot be compromised, and no weapon formed against it can stand.

Finally, if the above is indeed true, then Paul says we should live like it is so. Our next challenge is not only to believe it, but to live as though we trust it. There is a difference. Loving Jesus is one thing; loving Jesus and trusting him enough to live like him are wholly another. But when the chronic patterns of life seep in again, remember that *nothing* means "nothing." When we find ourselves facing the same giants and broken promises, remember that *nothing* means "nothing." When the world becomes too much, remember that *nothing* means "nothing." When the standards of expectations push at our sense of self-esteem and courage, *nothing* means "nothing." When the world screams in one ear and our self-doubt whispers in the other, *nothing* means "nothing." "Absolutely *nothing* can get between us and God's love" (Romans 8:39, emphasis added).

DEEPEN

Romans 8 uses several questions to provide a focused answer for us. One of these questions is, "What shall we say about these things?" It is the call of what happens when the world becomes too much for us. Do we give in? Do we give up? No. The answer is simple: "If God is for us, who can be against us?" (Romans 8:31 NIV). What do you feel is working against you—is it an attitude, a relationship, or a past mistake? What can you do to take hold of God's promises? The chronic life is about being stuck in the same old patterns to the point where they begin to define us. What does it mean to be defined by Christ's infinite love for us and by God's promises for protection? How does that reshape our lives?

DEPLOY

In Romans 8:31-39, Paul lists several items that cannot stand against God's love. Take each item and list it as a "category." Now, list specific details, situations, or circumstances from your life that fit into each of these categories—for example, the death of a dream or dealing with a broken relationship. Name the issue. How did this situation affect you, or how does it continue to affect you? Reread Romans 8:31-39. What is God's promise in the midst of brokenness? Follow this process for each category, and then watch how God works over the coming days and weeks. If the promise is true, then "nothing" separates us from God's love—we just have to remember that. God does. Do we?

DISCERN

Pray: *Gracious God, when you say "nothing will separate us from you," you mean "absolutely nothing"! We are so grateful for a God who has made the boundaries so clear and promised to protect us along the way. Give us courage to trust you and help our brothers and sisters know that even in the worst situation, nothing can separate us from your love. Amen.*

DAY TWENTY-SIX: "UNADORNED CLAY POTS OF ORDINARY LIVES"

Scripture: Read 2 Corinthians 4:5-13.

DISCOVER

SHANE: In my book *When God Disappears*, I shared the story of my friend Carol. Carol suffered from a chronic illness that over time made her body weaker and weaker. She would go through a difficult period, rebound, be OK for several weeks or even months, and then relapse. We played this scenario out several times over a couple of years until one day, in a hospital room, Carol didn't have to do it anymore. She passed away with her family at her bedside. I remember thinking on the drive home, *I hate death.* But as much as I hated death, I hated *dying* even more. There seemed to be something wrong, something so contrary to what the God I loved intended, in the way life can appear to be wasted as we transition from one place to another. And I hated dying because of what it does to those who remain after their loved ones are gone. With a world so wired together, dying seemed so out of place in the grand scheme of eternity.

As I drove, I realized that I was angry, but I wasn't sure at what. At first I was angry because of Carol's dying, but what I was feeling grew and became something more. I thought about how many times Carol had wanted to be "normal," to just have a day when she didn't have to worry about taking medicines or feeling bad. What she would have given to simply feel better— not just physically, but to feel certain, even for a few moments, that everything was worth it. I got angry for Carol and for me and for everyone else who gets up every day and refuses to give in, even when we secretly suspect that giving in might be easier.

Halfway home, I stopped at a mini-mart to get gas. As I waited to pay at the counter, I stood behind a young mother and her daughter. I was not in the best frame of mind and, like many of us, watched people too carefully, passing judgment on the way they dressed, spoke, or acted. The child in front of me was maybe four years old, beautiful but disheveled. Her green eyes caught my blue ones, and we looked at each other and smiled. I remembered that Carol had green eyes, eyes that were finally shut and now resting—that they weren't filled with worry and pain and tears anymore. For a moment, the young girl made me feel better because with the loss of my friend, here stood a new opportunity for life. Maybe this green-eyed girl wouldn't experience sickness and heartache.

Just then my daydream ended: the little girl's mother jerked the girl's arm and said, "Get up here; stop daydreaming." I noticed that the mother had placed a case of beer on the counter as she asked for cigarettes. "Colts, with filters," she said. She said more to the little girl, and though the words weren't mean, her tone certainly was. I felt anger rising in me again, but it wasn't about Carol—or at least, not all about Carol. I stood looking at the little girl and her mother, realizing that this little one, too, was in the middle of a chronic illness, but it had nothing to do with her body. She lived with a chronic parent in a chronic world, who didn't seem to get it or want it or even understand that they were dying without it. That "it" is hope and a future and real life. I was angry that while some were fighting to drain every bit from it before dying in a hospital bed, others seemed to be just going through the motions of dragging their "inconvenient" children around and missing the best opportunity for real joy standing right in front of them.

Walking back to my car, I counted—unfairly, I'm sure—all of the ways that this woman could do better and the reasons it seemed she never would—and why her little girl's life would be a sad by-product of neglect. She would likely grow up to repeat the same patterns and would miss the best things because she was consumed with the wrong things. (It felt like a long walk to the car.) I undid the cap on my gas tank and began fueling, convinced, rightly or wrongly, that I understood this woman's perspective and her circumstances. Anger and grief do that to us—blinding us from seeing the other side because "this side" is just too painful to muddle through.

Parked at the same pump was a huge, expensive SUV whose doors were open. Inside was a beautiful family. The father pumped gas while the mother arranged snacks and handed juice boxes back to each of her three children from a basket on her lap. The television was on, playing one of the latest children's movies, and all seemed right with the world.

Just then one of the children screamed, in a tone that would make my yellow Labrador puppy run up a tree, "I *told* you, I don't like *grape*!" She apparently did not prefer the flavor of her juice box. Her shriek was followed by a sibling's: "Mom, I *told* you, I wanted the *other* chips!"

The mother patiently handed the second girl another bag of chips, returning the previous ones to the basket. The first sibling continued to scream.

The father looked up from fueling and barked (in what my wife calls "a not too nice tone"), "*Give her the grape!*" The mother replied, "I'm doing the best I can!" The kid continued to scream. Like the mother in the store, the father said other words to his wife, words that were mean and hurtful because of *how* he said them. By this time, child number three chimed in because he wanted everyone to (in his words) "shut up!" because his movie had started. All the while, the mother continued to hand out drinks and snacks while the father pumped gas and fussed and the children screamed at their mother—and the world was not right! The mother looked over at me and smiled, but it wasn't a happy smile or even a courteous smile. It was the smile people give you when they would like to cry but can't.

By this time, the little girl and her mother whom I had seen at the counter inside the store earlier were on their way out. The mother was still dragging the child as they walked around the corner of the store, beer and cigarettes in hand. They had no car, and my best guess is that they lived in the trailer park visible just over the hill. I stood there pumping gas, wondering why it was taking so long, looking back and forth between the two scenes. On one side was a broken mother with a hurting child, and on the other side were broken children with a hurting mother. I thought, *Why can't that child,* thinking of the little girl from the store, *be with that mom?* I felt the impulse to stop the mother of the green-eyed girl and say, "Why don't you straighten up your act and realize what a blessing you have in that little hand holding yours? Put down that 'medicine' in the bag and spend some time loving the best thing you will ever know. Because I know a mother who would have loved to have one more moment with her child, and she wouldn't have spent it shouting or fussing or finding a way to forget her own misery." And then I wanted to turn to the SUV dad and the kids: "And why don't *you* realize what a gift you have in someone who takes care of your every need, and who loves you and cares for you even though you act like little brats and don't appreciate anything she does? Because I know a child who would love to hold her mother again, and not just to see what juice box or snack or video she could provide, but to really hold her and smell her and know that there is someone in the world who loves her best. And, sir, why don't you spend more time encouraging your wife and being thankful that she is healthy and here, and that she cares about how your day is going and making sure that your needs are met? Stop acting like she is your maid and your children's nanny. Why don't you treat her, instead, as the partner who makes your life meaningful? Because I know a husband who would give anything to hold his wife again and stroke her hair, even if it meant that he would have to spend every day taking care of her."

Just then, the pump stopped, and I realized that I had tears in my eyes. My hand gripped the gas nozzle, and my teeth were clenched. I replaced the dispenser, took my receipt, and got into my car.

As I drove off, the lump in my throat began to hurt, but not as bad as the hole in my heart. I thought about Carol, about Mike, about their daughters. I also thought about my own family—the times I had been good to them, but also the times when I had failed and forgotten what really matters in this world, when I too had gone through the motions of dragging around my family as though they were inconvenient. And I thought about those families I had seen today, about that unappreciated mother and that green-eyed, disregarded little girl . . . I stood at the tomb, and the hopelessness and disappointment and emptiness were too much. And so I wept.

The chronic illness is not always about our bodies. It can become about life and about our souls. And though the pain is different, it is all the more real and true.

Carol knew that we were incredibly ordinary people given a unique blessing: the next day. We learned early not to take the next day for granted. In forgetting this blessing, we too often miss what God has done, the imprint of his grace, and the gentle presence that feels like a gift. For those of us who have seen the other side of life's broken edge and trusted that even through the pain we can make something of it, life is sweet—every moment. Sure, we mess it up like anyone else, but we strive not to make the same mistake twice. We may be ordinary, but we know *extraordinary* when we feel it. And we want that feeling for everyone else, too. To miss out on this feeling means more than just missing the mark, it means missing the moment too. God loves that moment more than anyone, for it is where he amazes us, consoles us, and reminds us that we are not alone.

DEEPEN

Stories like that of Carol make us treasure life. Who is it in your life that you need to treasure? Who in your life have you perhaps not treated as you should have, and with whom you should reconnect today? Reread 2 Corinthians 4:5-13. Why is it so hard to follow the message God has given to us? Why do the distractions of the world find their way into our hearts and plans so easily? In what part of the story at the gas station do you recognize yourself? Are you one of the characters at the gas station? If so, which one?

DEPLOY

Tomorrow is never promised to us. What can we do to say "thank you" and "I love you" to those who matter most? Make a list of three to five people each day who need to hear you say to them one or both of the messages above. How will you let them know? Write down a promise to yourself (and to God) that you will not allow the world to distract you any longer. Allow God to fix the cracks and restore the "clay pots" of our lives to normal.

DISCERN

Pray: *Gracious God, you do not intend for us to live broken and distracted. Instead, you want us to experience life to its full measure. Lord, enter into our spirits and give us confidence that what you have to say is sufficient and real. We love you for loving us so dearly and do not want to dis-appoint you. Help us experience what it means to grab life and know the extraordinary work of your grace in us. In Jesus' name we pray. Amen.*

DAY TWENTY-SEVEN: HE KNOWS FROM WHERE WE COME

Scripture: Read Psalm 103:1-4.

DISCOVER

Each of us has children who love to play in the mud. They love to make mud huts, villages, and people. And when they are finished, they love to show us what they have created.

Mud is wonderful to play in. It has that quality that feels good between your fingers, and you have the impression that, given enough time, you could use it to make anything.

Over time, our children have become quite good at building with mud. Their houses and villages (along with the mud people who inhabit them) are far more complex than what we remember in our day. Maybe it is better "mud technology," or maybe it is just the skill of the builder. Who knows?

But one thing does not change. No matter how wonderful or beautiful the creation, once the rains come again—the same rains that helped make that mud in the first place—the mud village, the mud people, and all of the mud creations are reduced to chocolate-like fancies that don't resemble much at all. It is frustrating, but no matter how much planning a person does, there is really no great way to move the mud creation. Usually it just remains in place, and we live knowing that the next rainfall may be its last.

How ironic it is that we (all of Creation) were created out of mud. Just as the fertile dirt grows crops and minerals necessary for us to live and be healthy, we, too, were formed by the Creator from the mud, from the dirt of this earth. The essence of our existence is the earth, the mud, and that should mean something to us.

First, it means that we are connected to Creation in very personal ways. Those who question whether humanity should be so concerned with taking care of our planet should read the first three chapters of Genesis. The earth, at its muddy core, is as intimately connected to us as when God scooped his hand into the dirt and formed Adam.

Second, it means that for all of the complex ways in which we see humanity, our existence is set within the context of the rest of Creation. It is not an accident that we are not far removed from what happens in nature and Creation, and it is why God would put us in charge of its well-being.

But finally, our origins mean that we are intimately connected to one another. We are all most certainly cut from the same cloth, harvested from the same fertile ground, and God said it was good. But it became "very good" only when God made Eve and gave this muddy frame *community*. It didn't matter if we were plucked from the sky, formed from the depths of the sea, or raked from the soil, we were not complete without one another.

I believe that is why God is gracious to us in a couple of specific ways. He understands our origins. He knows the first steps; he understands that, like much of the rest of Creation, we are fragile. And we don't always get it right. But even then, God does not abandon us. He hangs in with Creation because he understands us.

The point is that God does not give up. He does not give in. The psalm says he revolves around our grace, wishing for the best but more than aware of the reality that as much as we want to, we will not always get it right.

If God understands this about our muddy frames, why can't we? Do you like living in the broken edges of life, or would you like to put the next piece in place and try something new? We must choose to reject the notion that all is "what it will be." God does not see it that way. Instead, he knows "how it should be" and reshapes our paths.

The chronic life is about patterns and relationships. But it is also about identity. These patterns and relationships convince us that we are not enough. And the truth is, we really are not enough. After all, we are just one step away from being crafted from the mud. But the psalmist says that God has made provision for us that we might grow to our potential, no matter where we begin.

Our goal for you is that you will not only remember your origins, but that you will celebrate a God who has not left us fragile, and who has loved us regardless. The rain can't hurt you now.

DEEPEN

It sounds strange in Psalm 103 to hear the psalmist talking about "blessing God" (see verse 1). But the word in Hebrew for *bless* literally means "to kneel." We are to "bless" God by realizing that we are not enough, that God *is*, and that God is working diligently in our lives to do something significant. What does it mean for you to "kneel" before God? How does that change your worship? your serving? your daily routine? The psalmist also says that God remembers our fragile origins. How does knowing that make you feel? What are God's intentions for those fragile places in your life?

DEPLOY

Find a time each day this week to physically "kneel" before God. Use this physical posture during your prayer time and personal devotion. How does it feel? Also, read Genesis chapter 2. Then grab some dirt and place it in a jar or a sealable bag. Occasionally take your hands and run them through the dirt. How does it feel? What does it mean to you to know that you were formed from dirt like this? How does that connect us to God and to one another?

DISCERN

Pray: *Gracious God of all Creation, we thank you that we are so intimately tied to your Creation and to nature. Give us an appreciation for how that connects us to you and to our world, and also to our brothers and sisters in faith. There is something so basic about having been formed from the dirt. Thank you for letting it be something that every day we can see and touch, and be reminded of its importance and simplicity. We love you for the majestically simple ways in which you work. Amen.*

DAY TWENTY-EIGHT: HE DID THIS FOR YOU

Scripture: Read Deuteronomy 10:12-21.

DISCOVER

DEANNA: My husband loves to work in the yard. In fact, some who know him would say that he loves working in the yard even more than he loves playing football. That is saying a lot! But it is true. My husband loves everything about yard work. He loves the equipment he buys, and he loves experimenting with new plants. He loves that he can work hard and then look back and see accomplishment. Unlike much of the rest of his day, yard work has tangible benefits where he knows he has done something.

Sometimes I watch him when he is finished, and he will just stand there looking over all that he has worked on for the day. He is a man with a very determined and proud expression. I can see it on his face: *I got to do all of this.* In many ways, he is like a little boy, using the yard toys to do some beautiful work. Nothing is more gorgeous than God's Creation when it is well taken care of.

Deuteronomy tells us that God loves to take a look back and survey all that he has done. God is proud of creation, even with all of our broken edges.

The writer of the passage in Deuteronomy 10:12-21 is vivid in his language about God's love for creation.

But the writer is also just as impressed with how God has taken care of other parts of creation. There is no part that God is not connected to, and God expects us to participate fully in God's plan. God wants us to treat each other with fairness and openness. He expects us to be respectful and kind, and God expects us not to take God's community for granted. After all, as the writer states, God is the "Master of all masters" (verse 17 *The Message*). There is nothing that has been made that God did not have a part in, because the very foundation of life flows from him.

Why is this important? It is important for a couple of reasons.

First, there is nothing upon this earth that is not traceable back to God and Creation. Even those things that have fallen far away from God's plan have their DNA connected to God's presence and work.

Second, because of that, all things come under God's authority. Each human being, each force, good or bad, comes under the responsibility of God's plan and will. God has created this world for his pleasure, to turn around and see the handiwork of his Creation. But there are flaws—not from God, but from us. We have not always lived up to what God's intentions for Creation were. In fact, we broke Creation, while at the same time breaking God's heart. But God did not throw Creation away. He didn't rip it up and start over. On the contrary, God works with and through us to address the broken places. When we slip into patterns of chronic living, we basically say to God, "We don't trust you to order the Creation that you brought forth from nothing." But casting off those restraints and living up to our potential testifies not only to God's work in us now but also to God's promise of what we can become.

The writer of Deuteronomy says that God is personally invested in Creation. God gave his only Son for Creation's redemption and restoration. And that says immeasurable things to you and me about how much God loves *us*. We are not thrown away or forgotten. Quite the opposite, we are the treasure of God's Creation, the apple of God's eye. What you have witnessed, the writer of Deuteronomy goes on to say, God did for *you*.

DEEPEN

What does it mean for the writer of Deuteronomy to say that God has ordered Creation for God's pleasure? How do we fit within that sentiment, and what does that say about our value in God's heart? Why do we so often look at the world through distorted images and concepts? Why is it easier to dismiss God's goodness and love for us than it is to embrace it? Finally, what does clinging to God the Creator, as described in Deuteronomy, mean for our future? How does such a relationship grant us peace and content-ment—the majesty of Creation implanted into our souls?

DEPLOY

If possible, take a walk. Look at nature; really look at it. What is it that you see when you stop to take in Creation? How does Creation's "handiwork" speak of the majesty and greatness of God? Write down your feelings, and ask yourself this question: if God feels this way about the mountains and rivers, the birds and the animals of the ocean, then how will God feel about me?

DISCERN

Pray: *Gracious God of all Creation, we are amazed by your handiwork. Thank you for making us a part of what you have worked so beautifully all around us, and thank you for making us the caretakers of something so precious to you. But, God, forgive us when we don't take nearly as good care of ourselves as we do of Creation around us. We confess that we are just as important as the birds of the air and the fish in the sea, and that our identity, first and foremost, belongs to you and comes from your heart. Help us live as your special Creation and to trust that your love for us never fails. We are amazed by your power, gracious God, but even more amazed and in awe of your love. Amen.*

DAY TWENTY-NINE: GOD IS REVEALED TO YOU

Scripture: Read Exodus 33:21–34:7.

DISCOVER

DEANNA: I have thought a lot about what would cause people to hide themselves from others. Maybe they are afraid. Maybe the other person in question is quite critical, and so unveiling themselves to this person would be traumatic or difficult. Some people hide because they are running from something. Others hide because they don't want to be bothered. My family and I discovered "hiding" when the glare of the media became too much and it seemed that we couldn't do anything right except for launching the next day's gossip.

Too often, hiding is a part of the human story, emotionally, relationally, and spiritually. Hiding is what Adam and Eve did when God first realized what had happened in the Garden. "What have you done?" was God's question, followed by, "Where are you?" God knew the answers to both of these questions but wanted Adam and Eve to realize that they had started a trend new to Creation—hiding. (See Genesis 3.)

But what does it mean when God is the one who does the hiding or at least limits the ways in which we can see God? In our modern faith, with so much biblically that encourages us to draw close to God, it is hard to understand what the story in Exodus 33:21–34:7 says, and what it means for those in that time and place in their relationship with God.

At that time, the only emissary communicating with God was a Midianite shepherd named Moses, who had freed the people from captivity in Egypt. Periodically, God would call him to the mountain, and Moses would communicate with God. But Moses never sees God because God says that it would be too much, and that God's glory would overwhelm even Moses. To consider such power of presence is incomprehensible, and such is the struggle of even the Hebrew language to describe what it meant to interact with God.

But in this passage, after the original Ten Commandments had been destroyed through Moses' frustration with his people below, God does something extraordinary: God agrees to come out of hiding. Moses is allowed to see the back part of God's robe. It will be only for a moment, and we learn later from the Scripture (and as dramatically portrayed by Charlton Heston in the 1956 film *The Ten Commandments*) that Moses is never the same again. This had been humanity's best shot, if only through the servant Moses, to catch a glimpse of the Creator of the universe. Until . . .

Fast-forward a thousand years to a small town called Bethlehem. By this time, not only has the world not seen God lately, it has not heard his voice in four hundred years. But then a baby cried, the newborn infant Jesus, and God came out of hiding for good.

One of the "penalties" of living the chronic life is this feeling of hiding—hiding among our friends, hiding among those who care about us, and feeling the need to withdraw within ourselves. God remedies this predicament by becoming like us and by unveiling the divine in human form.

And so, the next time you feel the need to hide, to run away from it all, remember that you cannot hide from God. You are not supposed to hide from God. God wants to be in your place, to make the journey with you, and to show you the full measure of God's presence, God's most wonderful gift. It is, quite simply, something to behold.

DEEPEN

As you read Exodus 33:21–34:7, what words and phrases stand out to you that unveil God's presence and personality to you? How does this passage appear similar to what we learn and hear about Jesus? How does the passage appear different? Now, read the passage again. What stands out in terms of Moses' part in this drama? What does God ask Moses to do? Why does God ask these things of Moses, even after Moses had destroyed the first set of commandments? What does this "do over" mean for us, for the children of Israel, and for our understanding of God?

DEPLOY

Make a list of personal "Ten Commandments." How does your list differ from the traditional one? How is it the same? Now, show your "Commandments" to a friend. Garner his or her reaction. Does it unnerve your friend to think of an alternative view? OK, now "operationalize" the commandments. Which ones do you start with? Which ones need action now?

DISCERN

Pray: *Gracious God, we appreciate the glimpses we get of your love and grace every day. Help us not take those moments for granted, and help us approach you honestly with our needs and concerns. But, God, we also want more than to see just the back of your clothes. We want to look into your face and follow your guidance. Give us the strength and courage to stand firm in your presence and to soak in the vastness of you. Thank you for making this possible through your Son, Jesus. We love you. Amen.*

DAY THIRTY: IT'S NOT A GAME!

Scripture: Read Acts 19:11-17.

DISCOVER

SHANE: One of my favorite movies is *Leap of Faith*, with Steve Martin. SPOILER ALERT: In the film, Martin plays Jonas Nightengale, a traveling preacher and faith healer who has devised a very smooth system for getting people's trust and then taking their money. He uses the system like a piece of art and believes he has the perfect scam—until he enters one particular town where a young mother catches on to Nightengale's tricks. It doesn't hurt that Nightengale, too, catches on to the young mother, intent on changing her mind about him. However, the woman has more to worry about than scams; she has a child who is ill and needs help. Of course, the movie winds its way around until the child finds himself at the stage of Nightengale, the faith healer. Nightengale rejects the moment and flees the town. However, before he goes, he prays a genuine prayer of healing, probably, as he notes, the first one he has prayed in many years. Subsequently, the child is healed.

For several years, I hosted a television program called *Time That Makes the Difference*. It was a thirty-five-year-old religious program that had preached the gospel and resourced the local church. At no time did this ministry ever really ask for money, and we certainly did not profess a "prosperity gospel," the idea that God blesses faithful believers with material wealth.

But after I left that position and went back to the pastorate, I had people question my sincerity and my ministry because, as they put it, I had been a "television preacher." The general view toward those who taught on television was so low that the stereotype crowded out the reality. It took a lot of work to convince many people in my new congregation that I was not in the pastorate for any other reason but to preach the gospel and to share God's love and grace. While I was speaking with one particular person about TV ministry, this person said, "It all appears to be such a game with those folks." I listened, and this person continued, "But even preaching on TV is not a game. The gospel means something to people's lives."

I agreed completely with this person's assessment. Some pastors, regardless of whether they appear on TV, have reduced the Christian faith to a circus act or bad theater. But for these people, there is very little, if any, genuine feeling in it. Real faith is where the heart is changed; where, as in Acts 19:11-17, the demons run for cover; it is when the people of God begin to feel it. Playing a game of faith will not do it. No, *the real thing* is what is needed, and when people see it, they recognize it, and they don't want it to end.

The chronic life too often is filled with emotional and relational games. We play these games with ourselves, with strangers, and with the people we love. But God's love for us is not a game, and neither is the way God intends to change our circumstances. By taking on the real deal and trusting what God has offered, we find not a false hope, a stage show, or an act—we find *real* peace and contentment.

DEEPEN

Oftentimes, God allows "the game of life" to play out in us, so that we might see the other side of his grace. Why do you believe God finds this important in our walk? What does it mean when we see the "real deal" of relationship with God? How do those qualities feel different and give us strength? Why do you think people often are drawn to playing games in life? What scares people about being authentic? What are the blessings that come from living a genuine life in Christ?

DEPLOY

Write a brief stage play about your encounter with God. It doesn't have to be a long or complicated script, just an outline of a conversation between you and God. What does your script tell you about how you see God's love in your life? How does it speak to your own confidence and commitment in faith? Why do so many of us need a "new story" to tell when it comes to God's work in us?

DISCERN

Pray: *Gracious God, we don't want to play games any longer. We are tired of not being "the real deal" for you and for your people. Give us both the humility to live faithfully in the world and the grace to follow where you lead. Help us meet our brothers and sisters honestly in their paths and to work to bring all us out of the shadows and into relationship that really matters and makes a difference. Amen.*

CHAPTER SIX

THE CURE: ENCOURAGEMENT

SHANE: My third-grade Sunday school teacher was a short, demure woman named Mrs. Gandy. Mrs. Gandy passed away a few years ago, but not before she was able to attend my very first book signing. I looked up at one point during the event, and there, sitting in her wheelchair, was an aged but beautiful little lady with a huge smile on her face. Although we had talked only a couple of times in the previous twenty years, she seemed so proud of all that was going on with me. There is just something special in the bond between a child and his or her first Sunday school teacher.

Mrs. Gandy appeared in my life like an angel. She taught at the local Baptist church in the new community where my mom and I moved following my parents' divorce. Prior to the divorce, we had attended my grandparents' church, which was a small, rural congregation with great people but not a lot for children. Thus, my mother was very excited that this new Baptist church placed a high premium on children's ministries.

At the time my parents got a divorce, I had been through two major hemophiliac injuries. Thus, I was dealing with the breakup of our family's home, but also the pain associated with a bad hip and thigh injuries. When I arrived in Hattiesburg, Mississippi, following the divorce becoming final, my mother and I moved into a rather simple house on a quiet cul-de-sac. There were other children who lived on our street, and it was a great place to grow up. But this was also a difficult time, as it would be for any child going through such a life change. I didn't talk to my mother about the situation; she seemed consumed with her own pain. I was an only child, so there were no siblings to confide in. The only people whom I could tell anything, and did, were my grandfather and my father. But I saw them only every other week, at the appointed visitation hour. Other than that, there were no opportunities for counseling or for purging the emotions that I felt toward and for my parents' situation.

Mrs. Gandy seemed to pick up on this immediately. I have written before about Mrs. Gandy. She would meet her Sunday school students at the door of the classroom, and the games would begin. We had a great time learning Scripture, sharing in games and fun crafts, and also making our prayer requests. It was during one of these prayer-request times that I shared about my mother and father. Each of them was still very upset with the other, and to make matters worse, my mother was engaged to a new man who would be my stepfather. My stepfather would end up being one of the great influences of my life, but at the time all I could see was this man invading my life and my space.

Mrs. Gandy knew my stepfather; that helped. She had been his Sunday school teacher years before, and she would tell me that my mother was marrying "a fine man." But more than anything, Mrs. Gandy listened. I started arriving much earlier than the other children in the class and would think of reasons to stay afterward in order to talk with her. Usually,

I would volunteer to wipe down the tables or simply put away supplies, but Mrs. Gandy knew there was more to it. And she was patient with me.

One Sunday I arrived with a particularly bad heartache. My mother and father had been arguing over child visitation rights, and my father had threatened to file for sole custody. He wouldn't win, but he would cause my mom a lot of trouble. My mother, in return, said that she and my step-father would file for my stepfather to adopt me. That did not sit well at all with my father. My parents were hurting, and in the middle was me. Mrs. Gandy saw my predicament and spent nearly a year helping me to see the better side of what God was doing and could do, even through this situation. I remember Mrs. Gandy praying the sweetest prayers as she would invite God to give me strength and joy. I needed large doses of both.

As I look back now, I see that Mrs. Gandy was my encourager, the one whom the Bible says God provides when we face difficult crossroads in life. I never expected Mrs. Gandy to be an angel for me, but she was profound nonetheless, and I will never be able to repay all that she meant to me during that time of my life. Mrs. Gandy did more than understand my situation, and she did more than simply respond. She became my advocate. She "got in the dirt" with me, wrapped her arms around me, and made me feel safe.

Part of the chronic life is when the world prevents us from reaching to the next person—not for our sake, so to speak, but for the sake of those whose lives we are supposed to encourage. If you look at the life of the apostle Paul, you discover a life of encouragement. Keep in mind that encouragement was not necessarily his spiritual gift; OK, it *definitely* was not his spiritual gift. But encouragement is not about how we are spiritually gifted. Encouragement is about our place within the Body of Christ and about how we are all connected to one another. We are called to jump into the foxhole for and with one another, for no other reason than that is what God did for us.

While serving as pastor at the church that I co-founded, I met Ms. Betty. Betty was a lovely woman who loved life and loved her church. This new adventure in the life of a brand-new church was right up her alley. She loved every minute of the loading and unloading, the setting up and the taking down that go along with a new church just getting started.

The only downside in Ms. Betty's life is that her husband, a good but stubborn man named Bill, refused to be a part of the new church. Ms. Betty showed up to church events alone, and during quiet moments she would ask me to pray for Bill. "He is a good man," she would say. "He just doesn't understand why he needs this yet." I remember the patience but also the pain in her eyes. She so desperately wanted Bill to come to church with her. But he wouldn't.

The day that Ms. Betty was diagnosed with pancreatic cancer remains one of the worst days of my ministry. She was diagnosed with a particularly active and virulent form of the disease, and her doctors gave Ms. Betty less than a year to live. I visited Betty and Bill almost every day for the next five months, until one day, in her hospice-provided hospital bed at her home, Ms. Betty went home to be with the Lord.

Each visit had been the same routine. We would talk about all that was going on at the church, I would read some Scripture, and then we would pray. But after we prayed, Ms. Betty made me sing her favorite song with her, "O How I Love Jesus." I later learned that Ms. Betty had sung that song around the house for years. Bill liked the song too, but it never had moved him much, at least not where others could see it.

Just before Ms. Betty died, she made me promise that I would look after Bill. "He is a good man, Shane," she would always begin, "but this will be so hard for him." And it was hard. Understandably, Bill was a mess. I called him periodically for several months after the funeral, keeping my promise to Ms. Betty. But more than anything, I would pray and use our few conversations simply to encourage him. He was thankful for the friendship, if for no other reason than because, as he would tell me, "Betty loved you so."

One Sunday morning, some seven months after Betty had died, we were at the end of the worship service and were singing our invitational chorus. It was a beautiful song first sung by the Hillsong United ministry, titled

"What the Lord Has Done in Me." That song always moved people from their seats, and without fail it would move me to tears.

On this particular Sunday, I was standing at the front, facing the congregation with my hands stretched out to God. I was singing away, when someone caught the corner of my eye. I looked over and saw Bill making his way to the altar. He knelt (or collapsed would be the better way to describe it) on the prayer railing. I moved toward him and could see the tears flowing down his cheeks. But I could also see his mouth moving. At first, I thought he was singing the words of the chorus. However, when I got to Bill I heard a different melody: he was singing the melody of "O How I Love Jesus." I touched Bill's hands, which were folded in prayer on the railing. He looked up at me, and with a smile, he said, "She would be so proud today. I have finally gotten it. I see it, Shane. It is real." I could tell that he had indeed "gotten it" and that now he wanted others to know. I reached down closer to his face and whispered into his ear, "She is proud, Bill. Trust me, she is proud."

We are called to be encouragers. When we have gotten out of our own way, understood the dynamics, and renewed our minds for a new way of approaching the world; when we have moved from just loving Jesus to actually loving *like* Jesus, *then* God uses us. He throws us into the game, and we are to become no less than his star players. Encouragement is not about simply giving a "word of hope" or "good news"; it is about getting into the mix of other people's lives, praying for them, walking with them, and *never* giving up on them.

I have a friend who says that *no one* should ever pray alone, cry alone, or die alone. It is profound how many of those kinds of moments so many people bear by themselves. And thus, simply knowing Jesus is not enough. We must become Christ for our world.

Over the next ten days, as you set your spiritual focus on *encouragement*, you will learn about how we are tied together in such powerful ways that the world is unable to understand or describe it. Our prayer for you over the next ten days is that God will break your heart and give you the privilege of pulling alongside someone who needs your grace and strength to move forward. It won't be easy. Much of the world does not know how in need it is. And many people will only move away from your gesture, without knowing or understanding the full scope of how broken we all really are. But your job is to stand firm, to stay close, and to never move from the gap. You may wonder how in your own state you can become an encourager for someone else. The answer is simple: we become what we focus on. Don't worry; you are ready. *This* is what God has had in store for you all along.

Let's pray:

Gracious God, we have moved through the dust and find ourselves at your feet. We want so much more for our lives, and you have promised to give it to us if we will just trust you and follow you. Lord, we do trust you. And we will follow where you lead. Those are not easy words, Lord; in fact, they are quite scary. But you are greater than our fears, and so we move the doubts out of our heads and begin to follow our hearts. We are amazed. We are in awe. We are yours. God, make us advocates for our brothers and sisters. We need each other so much. Help us not miss the point—help us not miss you. We love you. Amen.

RECOMMENDED RESOURCES

Lucado, Max. *When God Whispers Your Name*, special ed. Nashville: Thomas Nelson, 2009.

Ortberg, John. *If You Want to Walk on Water, You Have to Get Out of the Boat.* Grand Rapids, Mich.: Zondervan, 2003.

TEN-DAY SPIRITUAL TREATMENT PLAN FOR ENCOURAGEMENT

DAY THIRTY-ONE: EMBRACING THE GOD WHO EMBRACES YOU

Scripture: Read Romans 10:8-13.

DISCOVER

SHANE: When I was young, I loved to go my grandmother's house. It was a vacation in every trip. I was treated like a king or, at the very least, like the favorite grandchild—a fact that my long-suffering cousins endured. They are true saints!

However, I never really thought much about it. I just knew how much I loved being doted upon and how much I enjoyed the pampering.

A visit to my grandmother's house would involve getting just about anything I wanted to eat, including the best pancakes I have ever eaten. It also meant getting to stay up late and watch movies well past my regular bedtime. Before my grandmother would say good night to us and go to bed, she would give us a huge hug with her little frame and tell us how much she loved us. No matter what indulgences I may have experienced during my visit to my grandmother's house, it was these hugs that I secretly looked forward to the most.

As I have grown up and matured, I now tell the stories of these visits often to my own children. I want them to know the joy of what I experienced, especially since they have grandparents who treat them like treasures as well. My children understand a grandmother's sweet embrace.

I also have realized the number of folks who never had this kind of loving relationship, not only with a grandmother but with anyone. They never had that embrace or unconditional love. Their early life was void of this kind of affection and emotion. Today, many of these people are very well rounded and do quite well emotionally, but I have never met anyone who would not have wanted to experience more affection and affirmation growing up. It's something that is so significant—having people love you so much that they "crave" to embrace you as a means of helping you know how much their love goes with you, and how much they believe in you.

Romans 10:8-13 is written to God's children as a verbal embrace of God's love, and as a reminder that there is nothing we can do to separate us from God's affection. And when things are troubling or difficult, everyone who calls out to God is heard. What an incredible promise! What an incredible fact! The God of the universe not only "knows" you; he continues to reach out to you and embrace you. His love neither fails nor stops growing. He has set everything right between us, so that we might draw close to him without hesitation and find him faithful.

DEEPEN

In Romans 10:8-13, what does it mean that the "word that saves is right here, as near as the tongue in your mouth, as close as the heart in your chest" (verse 8)? What does this mean for God's embrace of us? What does it mean that God will "respond" to all who call out to him? How does God respond? How has God responded in your life? The Scripture says that "no one who trusts God like this—heart and soul—will ever regret it" (verse 11). What does this mean in real terms for those who have never felt the embrace of a loved one? What does this mean in terms of understanding God's love for us?

DEPLOY

Think of two or three people who need your "embrace" today. How can you emotionally or relationally embrace those in need today? Sending a note or making a phone call might be two examples; what other examples can you add? "Embrace" someone in need in the love of God today, and later think about his or her response and how it made you feel.

DISCERN

Pray: *Gracious God, you have drawn close to us that we might know you better. You embrace us with the love of a grandmother or a doting parent. We thank you for your affection for us and for how you call us to share that with others. The chronic life is about isolation. You are about opening us up to grace and hope in relationships that fill the voids and give us a new way to see the world. Help us not miss that embrace, that word of grace, or that smile that will make the difference, and help us share you with the world today. Amen.*

DAY THIRTY-TWO: INFUSED WITH STRENGTH FOR THE DAY

Scripture: Read 1 Thessalonians 5:6-13.

DISCOVER

Recently we heard the story of a pastor who was appointed to a church with a fairly large congregation, probably two thousand people. As the pastor was going through the interview and appointment process, there was little mention of things the congregation had experienced years earlier that would, for a generation or two, create significant dysfunction in the church's life. But much had happened to this church over the previous few years. Not only had they had three pastors in five years but also they had experienced significant turmoil among the membership. The problem was, in interviewing the new pastor, the church failed to mention these facts out of fear that he might not take the job.

Within the first weeks after his arrival, his tires were slashed over a disagreement with the son of a disgruntled and dismissed staff person. In a separate incident a few days later, someone urinated on his sofa and poured water on his computer. This was certainly not a great start. Before long, the pastor started getting hate mail.

After two months at the new church, the new pastor was convinced that he had made a mistake. Who wouldn't have considered that? It was a difficult time, as he grew more concerned about this decision, particularly as it related to the health of his family. He had dealt with difficult moments before but never anything like this.

At the previous church, the new pastor and his family had been involved with the same discipleship group for almost nine years. They had become very close and had covenanted to take care of one another no matter the circumstances. The pastor's former discipleship group heard about the difficult transition he was now experiencing, and they began praying for him and his family, and calling them every day. If they couldn't be there, they felt, then they would commit themselves to providing "prayer cover," as they called it. They checked on the pastor daily, reminding him of God's love. Though these special people in his life were far away now, they drew close to him in other ways.

This group infused the pastor with strength to stay the course and the moral certainty not to retaliate but to love. It would have been easy to get in the dirt with those who wanted him to leave, but that would not have witnessed to God's grace, nor would it have proclaimed a new day for the congregation. No, this congregation needed stability. The situation was pushing them to the limits no doubt to see if the pastor and his family would hold fast to what they said they believed. But when the pastor's armor began to crack, God sent his friends and family to instill in him the needed courage and strength to stand.

The Scripture passage in 1 Thessalonians 5:6-13 is clear, especially for those who feel the pains and pressures of the chronic life. When we offer encouragement, we do more than lift up a friend—we instill in that person the strength to face the next day. These were more than friends; these were witnesses, grace- and love-generators who gave the energy to keep preaching, loving, and living the faith.

God loves offering us the gift of godly friends who watch out for our well-being. They are "generators" of grace who protect us from the bruises of wounded relationships and people. And even as we are standing firm against these struggles, God will give us the energy to go deeper and lead others there as well.

DEEPEN

Think about the following question either through the lens of your own experience or by putting yourself in the place of someone else: What does it feel like to be mocked and persecuted for your faith? Why do such emotions drain us so deeply in our work? Why do these interactions hurt our hearts and souls so deeply? How does God offer us a new start and the strength not only to endure but also to prevail? Why do healthy covenant friendships make such a difference in our lives and in our faith?

DEPLOY

Make a list of your love- and grace-generators, those special people in your life with whom you share a mutually supportive bond of encouragement and love. Which persons on your list need a word of encouragement from you today? How can you consistently be in fellowship with them?

How can you make the encouragement of friends and family a consistent part of your spiritual practices?

DISCERN

Pray: *Gracious God of relationships, you created us to need one another. You called us into relationship with you and then deployed us to be in relationship with one another. Give us the grace to live this faithfully. Not only do we need it, but others need this reminder through us as well. Make us faithful in the practice of Christian courtesy and hospitality that no matter the situation, we will always have that voice that cheers us on and never lets us forget about what you have done and what you mean to each of us. We love you. Amen.*

DAY THIRTY-THREE: SAFE DRIVING

Scripture: Read James 1:19-27.

DISCOVER

The young woman now understood the importance of road signs, especially as the train roared past her only feet from the front of her vehicle. She looked in the backseat and saw her young daughter sleeping in her car seat, unaware of what had almost happened.

The young mother had been looking down, trying to reach her cell phone, which had fallen to the floorboard of her SUV. She had not seen the sign indicating a train crossing just around the sharp curve. This was an unfamiliar road, and though she considered herself a good driver, she never had traveled this particular road before, and it was dangerous enough without the added problem of not paying attention.

But she had looked up just in time to see the crossing gates lowered. She slammed on her brakes, coming to a stop just under the long arm of the gate. The force and power of the passing train rocked her vehicle. But even with all of the noise of the train and the violence of it racing by, the woman's car was in no danger. She had stopped "just in time."

The woman took a deep breath, looked back for a second time at her sweet, sleeping baby, and said a quick prayer of thanks. She also vowed never again to reach down for anything while her car was moving; the risks for her and, more important, for those she loved were too much.

In James 1:19-27, the writer, James, warns the reader about the dangers of life's journey. He says we too often hear what we want to hear instead of listening for the lessons we need in order to live better and healthier. It is just easier, James insists, to believe the lie than to trust the truth, especially if the truth requires much effort from us.

And so we convince ourselves that it is OK to take our eyes off the road. We look to everything but the path ahead, and in the blink of an eye, we can find ourselves in great jeopardy. Looking anywhere but straight ahead can be dangerous.

For many in the clutches of chronic, unhealthy patterns, we learn to talk a good game, to look everywhere but where our attention is needed. Sure, we may learn to navigate the road fairly well, but it only takes one moment.

James says the answer to such a life is to stick to the basics. Just as driving a car is safest when our eyes are on the road and both hands are on the wheel, it is critical that we keep our lives moving ahead, on the path, making good decisions and using our gifts to help others. Any other pattern steers us away from our destination and makes the journey all the more difficult.

How is your journey going? How many accidents and crashes have you experienced because you took your eyes off the most important aspects of life? Don't kid yourself. We can only do so much of life "off the cuff." The trip goes smoothest when we find the right path, watch for the curves, and keep life at a decent, manageable pace. And along the way, we should help others do the same.

James says that we should "act on what we hear." But we should also make sure to "hear how we act" so that we will notice the guardrails and stop in time.

DEEPEN

Read James 1:19-27 again. Listen to the intensity in James's voice as he describes the real purpose of faith. Why does faith go off track so easily? What is the answer to misguided faith and making a difference for Christ? Do you know of someone who "talks a good game"? What is that person like? What does a person who "walks the walk" look like in James's eyes?

DEPLOY

Read the version of James 1:19-27 in *The Message*. Make a list of the body parts used to describe sharing the faith. Why does James use these parts? And what does each part mean for us as we go forward proclaiming the Good News? What do you expect from your church experience? Does your current body of faith meet those needs?

DISCERN

Pray: *Gracious God, thank you for drawing us close to you and for filling the integral parts of our lives with renewed passion. We love that you have made us faithful for participating in your plan. But we do not want to be practitioners of "hot air" religion. We want to be genuine and to make a difference in our world. Give us grace, wisdom, and skills to do just that. We want to serve you. We are yours. Amen.*

DAY THIRTY-FOUR: THE HEAVY LIFE MADE LIGHT

Scripture: Read Lamentations 3:19-30.

DISCOVER

SHANE: In my book *You Can't Do Everything . . . So Do Something*, I shared a story about a mission center the church I founded started in late 2004. The congregation named the new center The Lighthouse. I'll admit the name was not my favorite, but the members of the church loved it.

The name conveyed the purpose of the facility, built by the congregation to minister to the under-resourced of the community through a food pantry, clothes-donation closet, life skills programs, and various other ministries designed to give persons in need dignity, hope, healing, and a new direction while navigating the jagged rocks of life.

Today, The Lighthouse provides services for hundreds of families per week and has become a powerful symbol of hope in the small community I served. However, as is so often the case, there was a story behind the story. The land where The Lighthouse sits was donated by a family who, at the time of the center's launch, were new to the congregation. We made the announcement that we were looking for a site to host our new missions center, and this particular family offered to donate the land to the church. It was a perfect location for our mission center.

The lot wasn't much to look at, with overgrown trees and brush in the front of the property. At the back sat an abandoned concrete slab where the old family home once existed. This land also had been the site of a tragedy.

The eldest daughter of the family told me the story of how their father, an abrupt, abusive man, repeatedly had beaten and tortured their mother, until their mother had found the strength to leave, the children with her. Over the years, he slipped back and forth between drunken rages and short periods of lucid sobriety. The children did their best to care for him, but ultimately he would hurt them with words and actions, and did everything in his power to push them away. Of course, he would beg their forgiveness, until the next time . . . and there was always a next time. This pattern continued until the children were in college, where they found their own lives apart from their father's desperate, broken cycles.

One spring morning, the eldest daughter received a call from her father, asking her to come by the house. She protested, but after much pleading from her father she eventually promised to be at the house around noon.

Little did she know that her father was asking her home not for a visit, but to witness an unspeakable horror. When she drove into the driveway, she noticed her father standing in the doorway of the house. He had soaked himself, the porch, and the rest of the home in gasoline. As the woman prepared to step out of her car, she watched as her father ignited himself and the house. The house exploded into flames, and in an instant both the man and the house were gone. Nothing remained but a pile of rubble on the concrete slab.

For nearly two and a half decades afterward, the family left the property alone, as it became overgrown in the debris of foliage, legend, and bad memories. They refused to do *anything* with the property. It simply sat there unoccupied and unused for nearly twenty-five years as a symbol of horror and pain.

Thus it was remarkable that the family, hearing our church's need for a site for our new missions center, agreed that God wanted them to give the property to the church. As the eldest daughter signed over the deed to the church, she said, "We agree that the devil has had this property long enough. It is now time for God to do something beautiful with it."

Several of us from the missions center team gathered with the family and took a picture on the newly mowed property as we held our shovels to break ground for a place that would ignite a new kind of fire, one born from the heart and grace of God. It was a beautiful, moving day.

That evening after the festivities, the mother of this family brought a gift to the church. It was a large square box that I could tell had been stored away for many years. She had left it at my door with a note taped to the side. It read: "In this box is the only thing we were able to save from the rubble of the house after the fire. I have had it in my attic all of these years waiting to see what God would do next. We have prayed that God would transform our pain into something that could be helpful for those whose lives have been battered and beaten by life. I hope you enjoy it."

I took the box home and opened it on the dining room table. What I pulled out was a worn-but-beautiful oil painting, still in a gold-leaf frame but with black soot marks along the edges. As I turned the painting around to look at the front, the image literally caused me to lose my breath: it was a picture of a lighthouse.

There are no coincidences in God's plan. And God's plan is for our lives to mean something, even as the flames brush against our hearts and souls. What we experience in the chronic life is not "normal." God has something more precious, more complete in store for us. His goal is to make the heavy life *light*. How? By helping us find more about who we are—and whose we are. And that picture makes all the difference.

DEEPEN

Reread Lamentations 3:19-30. The prophet Jeremiah is the writer here, and his spirits were down. Why? How did he express his struggle with God's plan and the way people responded to what he had proclaimed? However, by the end of the passage, Jeremiah's attitude had changed. What was the change? How did he express himself? How does Jeremiah's "journey" speak to our own spiritual journey, especially when God calls us into difficult relationships, places, or tasks?

DEPLOY

Make a list of your life's disappointments. It is time to turn these over to God—you have lamented over them long enough. How would Jeremiah suggest we "hand over" our disappointments and the heaviness of life to God? What keeps us from starting this process?

DISCERN

Pray: *Gracious God of new beginnings, you never meant for us to hold on to our disappointments. Quite the contrary, you sent Christ to put our lives together again and to help us see the real meaning of life. God, help us trust one another as we trust you and hand over the fragile places of our lives so that we might experience the "lightening" of those burdens. We are no longer afraid. We have you. We love you. Amen.*

DAY THIRTY-FIVE: HOT ONE DAY, COLD THE NEXT

Scripture: Read James 3:13-18.

DISCOVER

SHANE: "Hot one day, cold the next." These were the words of the gentleman who approached me at one church-related book signing I was attending. I was caught off-guard by how he started the conversation.

He had watched the *United Methodist Hour* television program for many years and had always liked the program until I started hosting it. It wasn't my theology or even my sermon topics that he disliked; he disliked that I wore a beard. In fact, the first program he saw me as host, he turned off the show and vowed never to watch again.

But being an avid *Hour* supporter for many years, he was determined not to let my "unkempt" appearance keep him from watching the program. Besides, as he put it, if he closed his eyes and just listened to the show, my sermons "weren't too bad."

Then, on one of the ensuing broadcasts, I shared how years before, one of my medications had caused the skin on my face to become very sensitive and how I "broke out" into a rash in the area around my mouth, chin, and neck. The redness and skin irritation were not only uncomfortable but embarrassing. And I developed scarring from the rash around my mouth area.

To offset the appearance, which was bright red, I grew a beard to cover up the splotches on my face. Being a hemophiliac, I knew this was also easier when it came to shaving, since it was that much less face to cut or nick.

When the gentleman heard me tell the story, he was embarrassed and ashamed about what he had thought of me. In fact, he was so upset with his immediate reaction that he drove to Jackson from the Mississippi Gulf Coast knowing that I would be at this particular event signing copies of my new book. He had no special business to conduct in Jackson, other than making the four-hour trip to say to me, "I'm sorry," which he did. He waited in line at the book table for almost thirty minutes, and then, after placing his books in front of me, he told me the "rest of the story" and asked for my forgiveness. I got up from behind the table, told him that he was most certainly "forgiven," and gave him a hug.

The gentleman continued as a regular fan of the program and a new friend of mine. His words that day struck me: "I saw you and immediately made a judgment call. I thought I knew your kind." He paused and then looked back at me, "But what I really saw was the 'kind' of Christian, brother, and man I had become . . . and I didn't like it."

We know the rules: "Don't judge a book by its cover" and "Don't judge a face by its hair"; OK, I made that second one up. But you get the picture: there is always more to the situation than we know or presume, and it will always benefit us to hear the rest of the story.

As Christians, we have a special duty *not* to jump to conclusions. Paul, Peter, John . . . even Jesus warned against making assumptions about our brothers and sisters before we know the whole truth.

The Body of Christ should be the one place where everyone is truly presumed innocent before any consideration of guilt.

My challenge for each of us in the Body of Christ is to talk with one another before we presume on someone's intentions, to ask questions before we assume on someone's purpose, and to seek understanding before we consume on someone's weakness. It will make all the difference, save us much grief in the future, and bring us, ever quicker, to the real business of living as "the hands and feet of Jesus" in this world.

James's primary purpose for this Scripture passage in 3:13-18 is not only that we have our eternal futures change, but that we learn what it means to live the abundant life as well. This life is full, as James says, of wisdom and grace. And we are called to be consistent in this life, not "hot one day, cold the next." The conniving, too-human life of trying to watch out for number one and always protect our own self-interests is replaced by Christ's example lived freely in faith. As this becomes our "station in life," we build a community around us that models what Christ has done for us. There is nothing more Christlike than to reframe our faith journey in a way that others may trust and follow themselves—no matter what people may think or perceive. Remember, God always knows our hearts, and that is the only measure that matters.

DEEPEN

When people talk about you, how does that make you feel? How do you normally respond? If you retaliate when you feel you are under criticism, what good comes from that reaction? What if you act like Christ—how does this reframe your example for God's people to witness? James 3:13-18 is about a life of grace and wisdom prepared and used by God for good things. What keeps us from achieving that life? How do we "walk back" toward God's intentions for our lives even among great scrutiny and critique? In keeping our eyes on Christ, James says we not only change ourselves; we change those around us.

DEPLOY

Make a list of persons who might need a word of encouragement from you to continue the race. It may be a pastor or a worker in your church who has grown tired and weary. It may be a friend who is dealing with medical problems. Or it may be a person who feels far away from God, someone who needs a new example of how we can meet the world and live better, more holy and faithful.

DISCERN

Pray: *Gracious God, we hear time and time again that our faith is not just about us, but about all those whom we will meet and serve. Help us not take this privilege for granted. We desperately need you, but not that we might keep you to ourselves. We want to "give you away" through our words, actions, and relationships, so that a community of the faithful is born. Forgive us when we have so arrogantly assumed that we can do it on our own. We can't. Help us, that we may live as you have intended. We want to live like you. Amen.*

DAY THIRTY-SIX: WHEN GOD'S PEOPLE BREAK YOUR HEART

Scripture: Read Mark 9:9-29.

DISCOVER

SHANE: Years ago at a conference for HIV/AIDS, I worked as a volunteer for the organizing committee of the conference, and it was my job to assist a prominent minister, who was a speaker for the conference, during his stay. Although this was our first encounter, I had heard bits and pieces of his story for several years. He was a multi-term president of a large Christian denomination. He had pastored a large, growing congregation viewed by many as a flagship church.

He provided leadership for his church on a national level during times when his denomination struggled with difficult issues, most notably the civil rights movement and the battle over biblical inerrancy. But nothing could prepare him for how his life and ministry would change in the early 1980s, when his son informed him that his daughter-in-law while pregnant with her first child, had contracted HIV through a blood transfusion. Following the birth of his second grandchild, the family discovered not only his daughter-in-law's HIV-positive status, but that both children also tested positive for HIV. The infant died that year, and his daughter-in-law died a few years later. His oldest grandson lived until the age of thirteen. The disease devastated the family, but it was the church that broke their hearts. After his son learned about his wife's condition, he immediately shared the news with the senior pastor of the congregation where he served as an associate pastor. The church fired him the next day.

This was a different time in so many ways than what we experience now in regards to HIV/AIDS. People were frightened and unsure about how transmission of the disease took place. They also struggled with many of the surrounding issues of the disease, particularly its connection to the homosexual community. Thus, for many well-meaning Christians, the issue paralyzed them from the inside out. And this fear was very real. People's lives were in danger because of irrational approaches to the disease. Children were turned away from schools, houses were firebombed, and people lost their jobs without any cause. And unfortunately, among the sinners was the church, who slowly, painfully, came to grips with the disease but only after a long and arduous journey.

Over the next few months, after relocating to another city and state, the family struggled to find child care, schools for the children, and even a church home because people's fears about the disease caused them to keep the family at arm's length. My colleague's son, while reeling from the loss of his family one member at a time, grew disillusioned over the course of the passing months and years, not only with the church but with the Christian faith in general. He was convinced, as he told his father, that the church was "just like any other business." Today he practices Eastern religion, having left Christianity altogether.

My colleague shared his story with me as we moved from one event to another at the HIV/AIDS conference. I sat in stunned silence—not at the devastation of the disease, for I understood the natural progression of the virus and its effect on the body. But even after everything I had experienced in my own journey as an HIV-positive Christian, I found it difficult to grasp his family's abandonment by the church. "What have we become?" I remember asking him. "It's not that we have become anything," he said sadly. "It's that we have become *nothing* to so many."

At that point, he told me about the final days of his eldest grandson. He had visited his grandson every week, especially during the final months of his life. He often asked the boy what he wanted to do, and the two of them would take off on some adventure. In his final days, the adventures grew difficult as his health failed. During one of their final visits, this brave young boy covered with tubes and confined to a wheelchair, asked his grandfather to take him to McDonald's. He always liked McDonald's, but to his grandfather, it seemed an odd place for a dying little boy's final adventure. But as good grandfathers do, he packed the boy up, and off they went to the golden arches.

When they arrived, the boy asked his grandfather to take him out to the playground. He was not eating much during those days anyway, and, as my colleague soon discovered, food was not the reason for the visit. When he wheeled his grandson through the playground doors, several kids made their way over to say hello. The boy laughed and talked like any little boy might do. As this man watched his grandson with the other children, he realized the reason for his grandson's last request: he had chosen McDonald's because he wanted to belong, and the children at McDonald's—unlike what he had experienced at church or at school—didn't care about his disease, his feeding tube, or his wheelchair. At the McDonald's playground, all little boys were equal.

My colleague finished telling me his story, and we drove in silence for several minutes. Both of us, men of the church who had seen our share of battles over this issue, still found the church's actions (or lack thereof) difficult to comprehend. And in the years since, I have experienced that awkward and sad silence many times—over different issues, but for the same reason: the inability of the Body of Christ to act like the Body of Christ.

"I guess I couldn't imagine a sadder experience in my entire life," he finally whispered. "Of all the places my grandson could have chosen to go during one of his final outings, he did not . . . he could not . . . choose the church." He looked into my eyes and continued, "He couldn't, because when they had a chance, the church didn't choose him." I couldn't help but wonder what Christ would have thought of this boy's final request. After pondering it for a moment, I concluded that Jesus would have driven him to McDonald's himself and had a ball with him and the other kids, all the while thinking about his wrong-headed, misguided followers: *You faithless generation . . . how long must I put up with you?*

How long, indeed? Much of our chronic nature spills out when we least expect it. We are to live as encouragers every day. There are no "off periods," no full exemptions, no exclusions. Hospitality marks and measures our faith in action. We don't get to pick and choose with whom and when we share God's love. The Bible is clear about this. The more encouragement we offer, the more we receive. One friend of mine describes encouragement this way: "Encouragement is God's fuel for the faithful life. The more we put in, the quality of its contents, and the ability for it to combust and provide energy and support mark the success of who we become in Christ." What a great image, especially as we become the encouragers for God's people. God expects nothing less than our all—our everything. This generation is counting on us. It is ready to go, but the question is, does it have the fuel to get there?

DEEPEN

In Mark 9, Jesus has confronted the religious authorities, the disciples, the crowd, and the father with the demon-possessed son. His answer to all of them is the same: "With God, all things are possible." What does that mean for you? Clearly, not all of our requests are answered. Therefore, what is God "up to" in not righting some situations, even though, clearly, he has the power to do so? What part do you and I play in helping others "face their doubt" and draw closer to Christ? Finally, what does this boy's story tell us about the power of fear and doubt?

DEPLOY

Think about people in your community whom some might consider to be the "lepers at the gate," the marginalized or the forgotten. Now, assess your part in helping meet their needs. How can you do better? How can you recruit and encourage others to participate as well? As we have said before, the chronic life is overcome by "getting out of ourselves" and going forward with something that means more than our illness.

DISCERN

Pray: *Gracious God, we apologize for when we have missed seeing your children in front of us and ignored the plight of those most fragile and vulnerable. This is not a "fend for yourself" faith. We walk along with each other, carrying each other's burdens if necessary. Help us not miss the markers you place in our paths. We don't want to "gain the world, but lose our souls" (Mark 8:36, paraphrased). Lord, we want to confront our doubts and the doubts of others, so that together, we might find you and also live like you in the world.*

DAY THIRTY-SEVEN: LOVE MEANS ...

Scripture: Read 2 John 4-6.

DISCOVER

DEANNA: There is a bookmark that is taped to my refrigerator, surviving most of our family moves. It is a simple bookmark. It was given to us by a young girl named Anna, who dealt with many physical issues. My husband, Brett, met Anna one season, and the entire football team fell in love with her. She gave Brett the bookmark, which included a scripture for the week and a saying or principle. We love this bookmark because it reminds us of Anna, not only her incredible journey but also the hope that comes from trusting in Jesus Christ every day.

A friend of mine also has a bookmark that he keeps on his refrigerator. It reads, "Love means . . ." I love that bookmark. At the bottom, it says that God gives us the opportunity to answer the end of that statement. Some days, love means patience. Other days, love means confidence. Some days, love means caring for those who are sick, while on other days love means listening and then sharing. There are days in our lives when love means putting ourselves after others. But there are also days when love means asking others for help. Love means . . . well, love means whatever we choose for it to mean in that particular moment. But the point of the bookmark is that every day, love means *something* in our lives. The best we are in this world will always have *love* in the midst of it.

There are days in our family's life when no amount of bookmarks with inspirational words will matter. We grow impatient with one another, sarcastic and tired. Those are not our best days. It is easy to tell the difference between when the day is marked by love and when it is marked by something else that is far less effective. With love, we not only have better days—that is a by-product of the power of love—but we have better relationships and better opportunities to show Christ to our world.

When I was going through chemo, I needed love each day. Sometimes I needed it to remind me of how blessed I was. Other days, I needed it in the form of someone helping me down the stairs. But there were other days when love meant getting out of bed and out of our ruts.

It is the same for anyone dealing with the chronic life. We begin simply by living what love means, by giving our best for each other, and by representing in words and actions that love is more than a concept—love is, as the Scripture tells us, the way we mimic God for others and live out his commandments. And this is the way it has been from the beginning—God's "bookmark" for our lives, if you will. And it says that God is consistent. As Paul says in 1 Corinthians 13:8 (NIV), "Love never fails," but it also never changes. This bookmark never goes out of style, and its message never gets old.

DEEPEN

After rereading 2 John 4-6, what does it mean for the way we love each other to directly reflect how we serve in the world? What are the commandments of God? How does love become a central part of these? What happens when someone tries to live out God's commandments without love?

DEPLOY

Think of one or two people who need to know the love of God. Send them a card or a note, or give them a phone call. Show them in some way what the love of God is all about. Why do we shy away from showing such emotion? What would the impact be if we were to make love the central framework for how we lived our lives and treated others?

DISCERN

Pray: *Gracious God of love, there is so much that we do not get right, and yet you love us anyway. God, we want to live like that. We want to know your grace and your love so deeply that they spill out of us and overflow. But we get scared, God, when we think of what that might mean for us. Break us; open us up. We want to be who you need us to be. We trust you. And we love you. Amen.*

DAY THIRTY-EIGHT: LISTEN

Scripture: Read Revelation 2:7, 10-11, 17.

DISCOVER

SHANE: I love to watch sports. Of course, I am fanatical about the traditional sports such as football, baseball, basketball, golf, and tennis. But, I have even grown to love soccer, rugby, and lacrosse. Each of them has a certain flavor about them that, even if you don't understand the rules, you can see the intensity and feel the desire of the competitors to win.

But there is no sport I have ever witnessed that is more intense than . . . curling. Yes, I said it: *curling*. Few people in the United States may even know what curling is, apart from its television coverage every four years at the Winter Olympics. But curling is a widely appreciated international sport with millions of followers.

Wikipedia describes the sport this way:

> Curling is a team sport in which stones are slid across a sheet of carefully prepared ice towards a target area. It is related to bowls, boule and shuffleboard. Two teams, each of four players, take turns sliding heavy, polished granite stones across the ice curling sheet towards the house, a circular target marked on the ice. Each team has eight stones. The purpose is to accumulate the highest score for a game, points being scored for the stones resting closest to the centre of the house at the conclusion of each end. An end is completed when both teams have thrown all of their stones. A game may consist of ten or eight ends. The throwing technique can induce a curved path, which may be further influenced by two sweepers with brooms who accompany the stone as it slides. A great deal of strategy and teamwork goes into determining the ideal path. ("Curling," Wikipedia, http://en.wikipedia.org/wiki/Curling [accessed June 25, 2010])

But what the definition does not tell you is that this ancient sport is ferocious in its competitive spirit. The teams, whose members typically look more like schoolteachers and accountants, turn into screaming, steely-eyed soldiers with brooms. As a spectator you are slightly amused at first as the teams are introduced, but once the game gets started, you sit with your mouth open, amazed at what these players do in pursuit of that perfectly positioned shot of a granite stone.

However, with all of the intensity, there is a moment just prior to the player's pushing the stone down the ice when everyone grows quiet and there is complete silence. This is the opportunity for the curler to make any course corrections. The team know that at this moment, they are to put their focus on him or her and listen. They can scream, holler, and roar into competition in a moment. But for now, let's listen and make sure we are together.

This is the purpose behind the Scripture passage from Revelation. God has brought everyone into a common thread of understanding. People know that God is at work and that the time of his return is very close. But at that moment when the roar is building to a crescendo pitch, the world goes silent, and God tells the church to listen—listen to what I have to share with you about your life, your potential, your resistance (which is coming), and the promise that I will never leave you.

This is the same promise, though, that God has made from the beginning. Even with our own personal lives spinning out of control and the edges seeming to unravel, God stops the action and says, "Listen!" We are reminded every day that we belong to God and that in following his lead, we are never alone. God is always trying to tell us something new, always trying to give us a better option for the life in which we find ourselves. But in the end, we have to be the ones who accept it, trust it, and live it.

Watch the intensity of God's love for you. It may seem unbelievable, but it is very real. We just have to listen for it and take it in.

DEEPEN

Reread Revelation 2:7, 10-11, 17. There are many strange phrases in the book of Revelation. Write down some of the phrases that seem awkward or unfamiliar. What is God trying to tell us about our relationship to him?

How is God speaking to our faith walk, our behavior with others, and our trust in him? What changes in our lives does this passage automatically insist must accompany the transformative love of God?

DEPLOY

Put yourself into a posture in which you are comfortable for prayer, whether it's lying on the floor, kneeling, or sitting. Once you are in your prayer posture, write down (in your journal, if you are keeping one) all of your worries for the day; be specific. Now set your list of worries aside. Take some deep breaths and clear your mind. *Listen . . . listen . . . listen.* What is God saying to you?

DISCERN

Pray: *Gracious God, we do not listen closely enough. In fact, we spend most of our time with you talking, either trying to explain our troubles, asking for help, or simply boasting about our accomplishments—that is, if we have taken the time to talk with you at all. God, we love you for your patience and guidance. You don't have to take the time to hear us, but you do. In fact, you crave it, because you have much to share. Help us hear, listen, and learn what you say to us today. Our hearts are open, Lord. Please speak. We love you. Amen.*

DAY THIRTY-NINE: BEGINNING AGAIN

Scripture: Read 2 Corinthians 5:14-21.

DISCOVER

Mad Church Disease: it is a surprisingly titled book that stops you in your tracks. One can't help but take a second look. Although not quite a best-seller, it has slowly built a faithful following.

The author, Anne Jackson, is exceptional in both her writing and her instinct for what happens when the church becomes a pastor's worst enemy. She detailed her own near collapse at the hands of the church she loved so much. As a pastor's daughter, she had seen the "family of God" act very unfamilial to her father and to her family. It not only left a bad taste in her mouth about church but about faith in general. After all, if God's people act like this, what about the God they serve?

The book describes how the church, being so invested in human beings and vice versa, has little choice but to experience the same ups and downs as any other organization or human endeavor. The problem, as Jackson details, is that the church is a volunteer institution, and thus has millions of "owners." Churchgoers don't see themselves as servants, but rather more as stockholders. This complicates the church's mission because everyone "owns" his or her local church. Thus, the focus has nowhere to go but inward. It is fascinating stuff, if only to a pastor. But it should be fascinating to all of us too, because what Jackson describes in the church is most certainly what happens in a chronic life in general.

For instance, no one gets up in the morning and says, "Today, I will screw up my life." Quite the contrary, most people, at least to a certain extent, want to make something of their day, to do good. But "good" is difficult to do when you are surrounded by the stresses and negativity of a world so off-kilter. The church is supposed to stand in the middle of this, but it falls victim to its own Achilles' heel—that in order to "be in the world," the church can be consumed by the world, too.

A person whose life has been dominated by doubt, pain, suffering, broken relationships, mistrust, and so on is at the cusp of collapsing under the weight of his or her own unrealized expectations. We want so much more, but it seems impossible to get there. This is not just our modern read on it, either. Look at any one of Jesus' interactions, and you will hear the same cries from those whose lives he touches. Call it "mad life disease." We are eaten away at the core, and by the time we realize how bad the situation is, we are no longer able to right the ship.

That is why God chooses a *"new* beginning" for us, not a refurbished one. We don't have to buy used parts to put our lives back together, we just have to be willing to listen and follow where God leads. In the Gospel of John (3:1-21), Jesus explains to Nicodemus what it means to be born anew, to be "'born from above' by the wind of God, the Spirit of God" (verse 8). Much like Nicodemus, we may find this idea of being born a second time hard to understand or even impossible. But actually, this is precisely the story of the good news of Jesus Christ, and it is the exact thing God intends for us through Christ. Through Christ, we are no longer on our own, but we are made part of one another because we are part of God.

The words in 2 Corinthians 5:14-21 are poignant. God has offered you something "new" and powerful for your life. The potential is unlimited. But you don't achieve it with your own gifts and skills. Instead, you find it in giving yourself away, and in trusting that with God what we need we have, and what we have is sufficient. *That* is the church—it's not some institution, but broken people joined together in an unbroken grace with a God who not only does not fail, but who also goes to great lengths that we might not fail either.

DEEPEN

Reread 2 Corinthians 5:14-21. What does it mean for one man to die for everyone? Describe the "resurrection life" (see verse 15 *The Message*). How does believing in it change our view of people? What does it mean for God to give the world a "fresh start" (verse 17 *The Message*)? How does that "new beginning" look in your life?

DEPLOY

On a piece of paper, write a "love letter" to God. Tell him why you want him to take over your life and give you a new beginning. What words do you use, and why? If we have been offered something deeper in Christ, how can you express it and share it? Now, take your letter and place it on a page in

a notebook or in your journal. On this page, write the words "The Past."
Then turn to a new page and at the top write the words "A New Beginning."
Reflect and talk with God about turning the page in your life from "The
Past" to "A New Beginning." It is that simple with God.

DISCERN

Pray: *Gracious God of new beginnings, your love for us is never-ending. Thank you for never
giving up on us and for providing a way for us to see and live like you through Christ. It is a gift we cannot repay and one that changes us forever. We pray that you will allow this "new beginning" to change
us, to change the way we see you, and to change the way we see one another. We love you. Amen.*

DAY FORTY: A LOUD "NO" ... A QUIET "YES"

Scripture: Read James 4:7-10.

DISCOVER

I have told the story of my friend Dan many times. There is no life that
exemplifies the message in James 4:7-10 better than his. At an earlier point
in time, Dan had lived an entirely different kind of life from how most of his
friends later would come to know him. Looking only at this earlier time in his
life, you might have seen so much wrong in Dan, so much that needed changing, so many characteristics familiar to the chronic life. But that was then.

Dan was a successful attorney, but he was not as successful at life. He
arrived at my office on a Monday and proceeded to ask for the best advice I
could give him about "why faith should matter." Dan wanted an answer
immediately. But I asked him to give me some time, and so I spent several
days thinking about what I should say.

The night before our next meeting, I awoke and wrote two phrases on the
pad sitting on the nightstand. The phrases were "Love Jesus" and "Love

Like Jesus." I couldn't think of anything more important for those of us who call ourselves Christians. It is not enough that we know Jesus and that we say we want to live like him. We need to put our energy into *loving* him, *knowing* him, *understanding* him, *becoming like* him. And then we put our energy into the world, loving like Jesus did for those who are the most forgotten and "the least of these" among our brothers and sisters (Matthew 25:40).

After sharing these phrases with my friend, I watched as his life changed. It was not my words or wisdom, but the simplicity of God working in him that transformed his priorities and his life. He began to read his Bible more, and he attended one Bible and life study after another. He became a regular attendee in the church and volunteered to serve in many different ways. He also joined a small accountability group that provided a new approach to community.

But that was not enough for Dan. After several months had gone by, Dan resigned from his law firm to take the directorship of a community ministry association that ministers to the needs of persons who are under-resourced. It was a huge life decision, but one that provided a new joy and direction for his life. Of course, it shocked everyone who had known "the old Dan," but those of us who had watched his life over the past months knew that he wanted more.

Over the next number of years, his life flourished and his work made a difference. Dan not only did amazing things in helping those in need, but he changed the spirit of his own life. And maybe most important, he changed the spirit of his family, friends, small group, and church. People could not help but notice what had happened in his life. They saw the changes where Dan seemed more at peace, more content; but they also saw the joy and the presence of mind in Dan that gave life purpose. Yet nothing compared to when they saw the results of what God would do in another person's life through the work of Dan's newfound career and motives. The more he gave his life away in service to others, the more he found the real meaning of his life. Dan's life had been successful, in a certain sense of the word, before; now, it was significant.

So what about *your* life? Are you happy with the status quo, with getting by, with the same routines that lead to lots of activity but few results that you cling to? Have you felt the pressure to be everything to everyone, but feel you end up being nothing or, at least, very little to no one? And when you do find something that gives you joy, excitement, and a feeling of purpose, how does that translate into what God really needs for you to accomplish, both for yourself and also within the Body of Christ?

The questions keep coming because this is about more than getting our calendars in order, getting our "to-do" lists straight, or deciding what our next volunteer ministry will be. This is how we are wired up. This is the way God has framed our beings. Apart from experiencing God's presence, *this* is what relationship in Christ is all about. It is the lynchpin of the good news— that Christ has transformed our lives and wants us to transform our world.

Friends, this is not supposed to be complicated. You have much to offer. God has gifted you—yes, you—and we want to help you discover that passion area and the way he has wired you up to accomplish significant things. It is the gospel imperative, but it is also part of your birthright as a child of God.

Faith in Christ is about more than just showing up at church on Sunday morning or volunteering to lead a Sunday school class (although those kinds of things are very important). It is about awakening the very image of God inside of you and then sharing that with the world. And—and this is a *big* "and"—as that is happening in you, others are doing the same thing, and the Body of Christ comes alive stronger than ever.

Someone once asked a small, elderly nun in one of the most depressed parts of the world why it was that, even with her failing health, she marched into the courtyard of the convent every morning to care for the countless people who were sick and dying and who lay on the makeshift stretchers. After all, she was far too old, some said, and surely she had paid her dues. After a moment, this wonderful woman of God (not unlike many we know with her love, doubts, fears, and joy for Jesus) looked and said, "Because this is how they will see Christ . . . and how I will see him, too."

That convent happened to be in Calcutta, India. The patients this woman cared for were AIDS victims, sufferers of leprosy, and others dying of diseases with no names yet. And the woman was *Mother Teresa*. She couldn't do *everything* . . . so she did *something*. And, well . . . the rest is history.

So over the coming weeks, months, and years, *love Jesus*, and then, *love* like *Jesus*. Go make history, my friend. The world needs you now.

DEEPEN

Reread James 4:7-10 in *The Message*. This passage is incredibly straightforward with its images of sin and purity placed side by side against each other. What does "dabbling in sin" (verse 8) mean in terms of your life? What does it mean, then, to "purify your inner life" and to "quit playing the field" (verse 8)? This Scripture passage also suggests that we must empty ourselves of us and "hit bottom" before God (verse 9). Can you describe what that would look like in your life? What are the benefits?

DEPLOY

If you have been reading this book from its beginning and following the spiritual treatment plan, you have spent a significant time—forty days now—reading, praying, studying, journaling, and serving. Now, simply get on your knees before God and pray the following prayer:

God, I love you. I am tired of living far from you. I want to be all that you have created in me and all that you intend for me. Make me holy as you are holy. Draw me close to your heart and heal me. I want to be whole. I want to be useful. I want to be yours. I love you, dear God. Give me Jesus . . . nothing more, nothing less, and I am complete. Amen.

DISCERN

So be it.

CHAPTER SEVEN

THE SEVEN WONDERS OF LIVING IN CHRIST

We often wonder what it must have been like for Moses to stand at the edge of the promised land and look over the horizon of the place he had dreamed of, a place he had spent the better part of his life trying to reach. We know that Moses, along with the rest of his generation of the Israelites, was not allowed to enter the promised land, because he and his people had strayed off course. But we can only imagine what Moses must have felt as he stood there thinking how close he had come but also how far away he still was.

You may know the end of the story. God felt so deeply for Moses that he backed Moses from the edge of the horizon, and when Moses died, God buried Moses personally, hiding his body so that no one would be able to desecrate the grave (see Deuteronomy 34). Even despite the Israelites breaking their covenant and promise to God, which had led God to forbid Moses from entering the promised land, what remained unchanged was how God loved Moses.

You may have become consumed with the worries of a life stuck in chronic patterns, but, friend, God loves you. God wants you to experience the wonders of a life much different from what the chronic life can offer. He wants to give you a new "normal."

When we get out of our own way and see the world from a new point of view; when we renew our lives by understanding the world from the inside out; when we learn to respond to the needs of those around us by faithfully loving like Jesus instead of just knowing him; when we become each other's advocates, stepping into the lives and hurts and habits of our brothers and sisters, encouraging them the way Christ encourages us, we go from "living chronic in crisis" to "living chronic in Christ." Before our normal was changed and before we realized all that God has in store for us, all we saw were the worries—the meaningless lives, the self-centered lives, and the uncontrollable addictions that led to patterns of poor decisions and broken relationships. But now, living in Christ, the result is that we no longer consume ourselves with the worries of this world, but rather we see the world from its edges of wonder. And unlike Moses, we get to go beyond the horizon and see the better parts as well.

What follow are the Seven Wonders of Living in Christ, unveiled.

WONDER NUMBER ONE:
HAVING GENUINE AFFECTION FOR OTHERS

The chronic life is about us. The life lived in Christ is about him and thus about others. Whereas life had closed itself off through chronic decisions and patterns that led to unhealthy places in our journey, the wonder of living in Christ connects us to others as God is connected to them. After all, Jesus says that "your love for one another will prove to the world that you are my disciples" (John 13:35).

SHANE: Ruby caught my eye the first time I met her. Before you begin to worry, Ruby was all of three years old at the time. Ruby was the big sister of a baby brother, whom I was baptizing.

In our congregation, the entire family comes forward when a member of the family is baptized. Since we baptize through the method of sprinkling, it is easy and appropriate for the family to stand at the altar. Ruby was more than ready to see her little brother baptized. So much so, that when the time came for the family members to answer the "family questions" in support and affirmation of the one being baptized, Ruby answered them all, and she answered each one a full second before her mom or dad. The congregation loved it, and so did I.

After I have finished baptizing the baby, it is my custom to walk the baby down the aisle to introduce the new brother or sister to the church family in the congregation. As I started to walk, Ruby grabbed my pocket and began to walk with us. At first, her mother said, "Oh, no, dear, you can't go with them," to which Ruby replied, "Oh, yes, Mom, Pastor Shane said it was time to introduce Alex to the congregation, and I need to make sure he is OK and not embarrassed." The congregation roared with laughter!

Ruby was intent on making sure that her little brother was OK. Her affection for him showed itself in many ways, but most notably and importantly by her simply wanting to be present where he went.

Real, healthy relationships are not meant to be complex or complicated. On the contrary, they are simple and lived out in love, grace, forgiveness, and purpose—affection poured out for one another, to build one another up and give hope.

We have much to learn from Ruby. Although she is just a child, she has no preconceived notions of what relationships should be. She doesn't work in a *quid pro quo* mind-set, expecting to receive something in exchange for something given. She loves her brother and has affection for him because he belongs to her and she belongs to him.

The same is true for us. We belong to one another. That is the basis of our affection. God has made us family, not simply acquaintances, and certainly not strangers. Whereas the chronic life separates us from one another, the healthy life, the one God has in store for us from the beginning, can't exist without this bond from you to me and vice versa. It is our relational, spiritual DNA at its finest. Ruby knows it. How about you?

WONDER NUMBER TWO:
FINDING REAL MEANING IN LIFE

We have watched over the past several months as so many people in the public eye, it seems, have been caught in one scandal after another. Watching their difficulties unfold, one would wonder what in the world they were thinking. Certainly each situation was different, but the central struggle was the same: at some point, they sought to fill the void at the center of their souls with something or someone who was not appropriate for their lives. Sounds simple? Well, it is.

That is not to say that the circumstances are simple. Absolutely not! There are spouses, children, loved ones, fans, and others who are involved emotionally, and some of them will never be the same because of these situations. But at the core of each situation was an illness derived from lack of meaning, and a person who decided to medicate that illness with "meds" not approved for his or her life.

The chronic life makes us feel as though we have to do it alone. Though God repeats that the emptiness we feel is not natural, we still try to make it well on our own. We spend inordinate amounts of time, resources, and relationships trying to replace the empty places with something, anything, that will make the ache go away.

Earlier in this book we described the "Seven Worries of Living in Crisis" and how the chronic life leads to a series of meaningless relationships and experiences. But having seen what God has in store, we know that meaninglessness is not normal in God's economy. God has meaning for everything—Creation, relationships, our actions, our intentions, you, me, everything—for everything flows back to him.

Where the "meaninglessness" comes into play is when we try to solve our issues on our own—which so many of us often do. This doesn't make us "bad" people by any means, even though the world likes to make us feel this way after we have fallen short in our attempt to steady life's imbalances. No, we are quite normal in our expectations that we can fix our fragile places with things of the world instead of things from God. But the results speak to the method—or at least its success.

On the other hand, a life lived in Christ craves meaning—real meaning that is not a facsimile of us but takes on the very image of Christ in us. Through a life lived in Christ, our marriages become stronger, our relationships are healthier, and our homes find peace. Does that sound good? It certainly does to us. So what do you say? Most of us have spent too much time living in other places; God says it is time to come home.

WONDER NUMBER THREE:
DEVELOPING A SENSE OF PURPOSE

DEANNA: It seems that many people think that daily life in the NFL includes spending your days being driven around in chauffeured limousines to the most basic of appointments, and that nothing goes by without help from some paid assistant. And that is just the spouses' lives.

Nothing could be farther from the truth. In fact, I am stuck in school pick-up lines much of my day, and I have the same long list of errands that most mothers or fathers probably have. And although we are fortunate to be able to have people around us who help with various tasks, most things around the Favre household remain our responsibility.

For me, I spend most of my time running to one event after another for our daughter. We are a blessed family with great children, but they keep us hopping, and no matter whether their father was an engineer, an accountant, or a quarterback in the NFL, their list of normal, daily expectations is much the same as that of any teenager or college student.

The same is true for Brett and me when it comes to our own personal goals. We have seen the bright lights of fame, and fame is not all it is cracked up to be. One evening after Brett had been on *The Tonight Show*, we had dinner with dear friends who are also in the spotlight. When the meal was over, I saw the gathering paparazzi outside the restaurant door and wanted no part of it. So as soon as the door of the restaurant opened, I ran for the car, got in, and locked the doors. I looked behind me to see if Brett was following and was horrified to see him still at the front door of the restaurant, surrounded by the photographers and reporters while talking to our friends.

When he got to the car, I asked him, "What in the world were you doing?" "Trying to say good-bye to our friends," he said with a bit of a tone in his voice. He was frustrated with the reporters, because we had not seen these particular friends in a while and had been looking forward to visiting with them.

Our goals and objectives for life are pretty much the same as those of anyone else—it is just that a lot of our life gets played out on the news, blogs, and websites. This has been evident in the series of "Retirement Watches" about whether Brett will play another season. But the decision to go back to football, to continue playing, was more about Brett wanting to prove something to himself; he wanted to address things that were unfinished inside of him. In his younger days, he might have responded differently, but as he has matured, he has taken all of us into consideration in making these decisions. We all have wanted him to keep going as long as he wants to and feels that he can play healthy and be successful at that level.

Arriving in Minnesota in 2009 was nerve-wracking but also exciting. For as long as he was a member of the Green Bay Packers, the Vikings had been one of Brett's biggest rivals, and he had not been liked there at all. But during the 2009 season, with hard work and dedication, it felt as though Brett won over the fans and the team, and he had one of his best seasons ever. And with the exception of a couple of rough plays in the last play-off game, it was a magical time. Brett played like a man on a mission that season, a man with a real purpose.

The chronic life robs us of our ability to make decisions and to focus our life's purpose in the right places. We become so consumed with "getting by" in life and being conformed to the mentality and goals of the world that we miss the chance to become all that God has in store for us. Our purpose is found in God's wonder for us, for our lives, for our families, and for our hopes and dreams. He does not want us to miss out on all that he has planned for us. We are his children, and that grace gives way to a life borne of his love and borne of his purpose, which never fail. And decisions made with those intentions may not be easy, but they are also never wrong.

WONDER NUMBER FOUR:
LIVING OUT COMPASSION AND CONVICTION

SHANE: One of my favorite books is a work titled *Three Simple Rules*, by Rueben P. Job. Bishop Job has been a leader in The United Methodist Church for many decades and is considered one of the foremost practical theologians in the world.

In *Three Simple Rules* Bishop Job says that John Wesley, the founder of the Methodist movement, believed in simple concepts that not only drove his theology but defined the way he saw the church working in the world. Bishop Job takes Wesley's words and condenses them into three primary rules or principles.

Bishop Job's first Wesleyan principle is "Do No Harm." Like its medical counterpart, this principle advises the student to first live a life that doesn't harm another person or provide an example that is detrimental to the goal of the Good News. As Bishop Job reminds us, we spend a lot of time living out examples that often do more harm than good. Our first goal, he says, is to live a life that creates an environment open to the Spirit of God and ready for where God will call us to work in the world.

The second principle is "Do Good." This one should be a given in the Christian faith, but Christians often have needed a reminder to participate in those activities that provide for as many open doors for the gospel as possible. We are to live our lives teaching, including others, loving, sharing, and serving in the name of Christ, and becoming with all of our hearts and lives "the hands and feet of Jesus."

Bishop Job's third principle is "Stay in Love with Jesus." This principle affected me most. The journey gets long and complicated, and it is easy for us to lose sight of whom we belong to and, especially, whom we serve in the world. The best way to keep our focus is to "stay in love" with the One who never abandons us and who gives us the best of himself through his Son, Jesus. In the book of Revelation, John reminds the seven churches not to forget their first love and to stay in love with Jesus (Revelation 2:4). Doing so protects us from our fragile natures and always keeps us focused on the right things.

The chronic life works against each of these principles. When life becomes too much about *us*, we forget our first love. Forgetting our first love makes doing good difficult; it's not that we are "bad" *per se*, but we are not living in the glare of God's purpose for our lives. And thus, the more we live in the shadows of the chronic life, the more harm we do, even when we are unaware of it.

One of the wonders of living in Christ is that we are reminded of our conviction. We are never let off the hook for it because God knows the real, genuine benefit behind it. If God keeps our eyes on him, then the Adversary has less chance to distract us and take us off course.

Everyone benefits from a life lived with compassion and conviction. Our families, friends, and relationships feel the freedom of a life lived for something bigger and deeper than us, and the result is not only a life of conviction but also real results that matter.

WONDER NUMBER FIVE:

ENRICHING LOYAL COMMITMENTS

SHANE: "Every marriage has problems." This was a phrase I had heard for many years in ministry, especially when I spent a couple of years in advanced training for marriage and family therapy. The more couples I observed in the training program, the more I understood this feeling. No marriage is immune.

I came from a divorced home. My wife, Pokey, did too. We knew about marriage difficulties, but for many years of our marriage we were experiencing what we thought was the exception to the rule. We genuinely loved each other, and with everything that we had been through, everyone believed that *nothing* could affect "Shane and Pokey." But everyone was wrong.

Soon after we completed graduate school, the Adversary, through a series of missteps in our marriage, opened a wound in us that would take years to heal. We began to live a chronic life.

It began with me becoming so consumed with doing the good Christian things that I forgot what it meant to be a good Christian husband. A church had rejected me as their pastor a couple of years earlier because of my HIV-positive status, and I had used this rejection as an excuse to begin unhealthy patterns of work. For lack of a better description, the church became my mistress, and the stress was too much for my marriage.

Pokey, on the other hand, found herself embroiled in a deeply emotional, unhealthy relationship. The relationship wasn't intentional; so many of these relationships are not. But it became a substitute for what Pokey's heart really wanted—a genuine, committed relationship with her husband. Over time the relationship, much like my own abandonment through the church, became complicated and nearly ended our marriage.

It was only after we confessed our failings to each other and then spent time working out our broken spirits that we found our way back together. Had the chronic nature of our lives won, we probably would have gotten a divorce. But the opposite happened. Not only did we put our marriage back together, but we have found life to be happier on this side of the fence than we had even thought possible before.

Was it a difficult road? You bet. And it almost cost us our relationship with each other. But the road also taught us about loyalty, honor, and purity in our relationships. Not only did we learn a lesson about our pasts, but we also made some commitments about our future. We would never again allow the world to define our marriage. We came out of the storm stronger than ever before.

The chronic life wants your relationships, plain and simple. It wants to break your heart and turn you off to love and grace so much that you are unable to recognize them even when God plants them deep within you.

A life lived in Christ experiences the wonder of a restored relationship by the One who made the greatest, most loving commitment to all of us. Nothing rivals what God did for us. In Philippians 2 (NIV), the apostle Paul says that Christ "made himself nothing" to give up everything and become like us. Why would Jesus do that? The answer is *love*, my friend. *Love*.

How does it make you feel to know that God loves you that much? Maybe it doesn't give you goose bumps or make the tears well up. But if your life turns upside down or your marriage nearly falls apart as we have experienced, then look around and see where the world is for you. It has long abandoned you. It will be a lonely feeling. When the smoke clears, you will find only one real face—Jesus. But rejoice and take heart, his loyalty, his commitment, is forever.

WONDER NUMBER SIX:

BEING ABLE TO MANAGE ENERGIES WISELY

One lesson we have learned from our friend who suffers from a chronic illness is that her day has a limited amount of energy for her to use. It doesn't matter how long she rests or saves her energy, as the day goes along her body will grow tired and her efforts labored. This is one of the most difficult things about watching our friend work through the symptoms and effects of a chronic illness. She is limited by the condition of her body. No matter how much she wants the situation to be different, she can't do anything about it.

The chronic life is like that, too. When we are living the chronic life, no matter how much we try, our relationships, our spiritual journey, and our efforts seem labored. There is a definite limit to what we can accomplish and even to what we feel like accomplishing.

The result is a life held hostage by the boundaries of our abilities, which are hindered, and by our spirits, which are wounded. By the end of the day, we wonder what can be done, if anything, to change these circumstances. And that is when the effects of a depressed and downcast spirit catch up to us.

I have known others held hostage by the chronic life who have not gone so easily. Their bodies can't keep up even with their own desires, and they soon run out of steam. The point of the chronic existence is to make the cycle unbreakable. Again, as we have said before, the adversary only needs to keep you locked up or distracted, not destroy you completely.

But when the chains of the chronic life are thrown off and we begin to live in Christ, our energy level changes. We see the world from a new point of view, and we find our old souls again. It is a joy to watch as a person comes "back to life," so to speak, and sees the world as new again.

One of the ways we watch people gain their lives back is that they learn to manage their energies wisely. In the chronic life there is not much to manage, or they manage their tasks with a broken spirit or body, ultimately leading to failure.

God has more for us. He doesn't want us limping around as if we have no better future. Quite the opposite: God wants us to run into his presence and to rejoice and dance, as the Scripture says.

SHANE: The life lived in Christ is a life full of possibilities. When our energies are sucked from us, then so, in many ways, is our potential. It is like the last time I saw my grandmother just before she passed away from cancer. She wanted me to bring her shoes so that she could slip them on and run in the grass. Of course, her body would not let her do that. After a few minutes, realizing her limitations in that chronic/terminal body, my grandmother turned to me and said, "That's OK, Shane. We will run together again someday, won't we?"

Yes, we will, Grandmother. Yes, we will. God wants us to run, not limp; to jump, not hobble, into his grace. We are built for dancing. God plays a symphony of hope and possibility for you. Do you hear the music?

WONDER NUMBER SEVEN:
CREATING SELFLESS VIEWS OF LIFE, GOD, AND GOD'S PEOPLE

We have a friend who is married to a lovely person, although she is consumed with herself. It is interesting to watch the couple's marriage. He is a good man with tremendous gifts and love for people. His wife is also a good person, but let push come to shove, and you know she is going to come down on the side of her own self-interests.

This attitude was ingrained in her from childhood. She was the younger of two children. Her older brother helped her parents make her self-absorbed. It is not that any of them are "bad" people. She is not a bad person either. But she is constantly focused on her own needs. And although age has made her responses more subtle, one still knows who is at the forefront of her thinking and desires.

It is sad if you think about it. This woman is beautiful, smart, and talented. But people quickly tire of her because she is so centered on herself. Her husband is either a saint or a fool, or maybe a little bit of both. Regardless, everyone agrees that he has done a disservice to their marriage by not requiring more from his wife—not in terms of duty or responsibilities, but an equal sharing of the focus and purpose for the marriage.

In the end, their life is their own. Many times we have said, "Well, if he is happy with that . . ." But we know that he really can't be happy with this situation. In fact, on more than one occasion now, this friend has opened up to me with some of his frustrations. *Nothing is ever good enough or in order enough. He never makes enough money, but he is also never home enough. He is never going to be enough because he can't fill the real void in her life: her own self-image.*

Again, our friend is truly lovely, but like so many of us, she is wounded in so many ways. She comes from a broken family with very unhealthy patterns of dysfunction. And she has brought these unhealthy expectations into her marriage. Her husband, who will never be enough, tries as hard as any husband I have ever known, but he cannot compete with the unsettled voices in his wife's heart. Eventually, we have decided, the marriage will become unstable, and we are afraid, it will be lost.

Covenantal relationships require give-and-take. They require a partnership. When one person is in control, the relationship cannot survive very long. The chronic life seeks to make it all about us. And the reasons are very simple. The more we focus on ourselves, the more we lose the ability to see God at work in our lives, and the more we lose the ability to watch how God can use us for others. It is a double devastation: we lose both our relationship with God and our relationship with our brothers and sisters by simply making life too much about *us*.

Living in Christ ushers in a new plan. The purpose is not a selfish point of view but a selfless focus. When we see the world from new angles, renew our minds, learn to respond and make a difference, and then become advocates for encouragement, we make life about others and not about us. It is not that we lose any of the joy or purpose. Instead, we *find* it, because we get ourselves out of the way. God wants us to find our lives . . . to win . . . to be victorious . . . to serve . . . and to be served. But the Scriptures are very clear as to how that happens. To be first, we must be last. To be victorious, we must be willing to lose. To be served, we must be willing to serve others. To find our lives in Christ, we must follow Christ's example and be willing to lose our lives instead.

But, friend, it is our choice to make. The blessings are evident and available. God sees our potential. God hears our cries. God calls us to something new and remarkable. Can we follow him? Can we lay it all down in order to do so? Do we trust him to be faithful to his word? Your answer, my answer, our answers to those questions can, and do, change everything. And it is in those answers that we find the difference between a life lived in crisis and a life lived in Christ.

AFTERWORD

Fred Smith is the founder and CEO of FedEx. Mr. Smith is world-renowned for his business skill, courage, and ability to create something from nothing. He is also the master of what most business leaders call the "conceptual leap"—the magical response to a problem, situation, or obstacle that leads a person or a group of people to think outside the box and to create a completely new way of achieving an objective, and in the process, developing a new approach to an entire industry or organizational practice.

The "conceptual leap" is the difference between repeating the same old patterns as before and embarking on new, untested paths that eventually lead to profound discoveries, changes, and achievements. What once was "unthinkable" becomes not only the "new idea" but *the* idea" that changes the way a group of people, a field of science, or an industry thinks about the way it does business.

For instance, how many people had looked into the deep, moldy remains of a Petri dish before Alexander Fleming had the conceptual leap that such contents could be used to fight infection? The result was Fleming's discovery of penicillin, which led the way for modern antibiotics and changed the course of health of the world.

Or how many times did the top pilots in the world try to break the sound barrier using the best-available aeronautical techniques and equipment, only to discover that a straight-winged plane could not produce enough velocity to make it happen? But if you redirected the wings at an angle, it was discovered, the air could move over the wings faster, still providing enough lift but also dramatically increasing the aircraft's speed.

What about NASA trying to send a person to the moon using the concept of a single rocket to be used to launch a crew and then return them safely? It was only when they made the conceptual leap to a three-phase rocket that the dream of landing astronauts on the moon and returning them safely became a real, viable possibility.

And then there is the story of some young people from the Pacific Northwest, Ivy League dropouts who believed that if you could standardize the viewing platform of computers into point-and-click methodologies instead of having to know complex computer code, millions of people could and would use a computer. That, along with the conceptual leap of the microchip, made Microsoft into a household name.

And let's talk about Fred Smith again. Prior to his conceptual leap, mail and packages followed a system of transport that could be explained as one-dimensional at best. But what would happen if you redesigned your delivery system from linear approaches to a spoke-and-wheel model using multiple forms of transportation such as planes, trains, and automobiles? Well, you create Federal Express and change the way and time in which packages make their way from one place to another.

Conceptual leaps, no matter how large or small, are the doorway to facing impossible problems with very possible solutions.

When we think of the chronic life, the chronic decisions, or the chronic patterns in which we often find ourselves, in the past we have done one or two things. First, we have assumed that the problem is about fixing the internal dynamics of the person in question. And second, we have believed that condition is merely bandage-able, not curable. Both are myths.

What we have learned from watching the chronic life in action is that, first, God does not consider the chronic life normal. And thus, he no more intends for you to remain in these patterns than he would ask you to remain ill if his healing touch was near. But second, God also knows that *we are not enough*, and that the healing takes place by removing the focus from us, not turning up the dial to make even the treatment one more part of the mis-shapen puzzle. On the contrary, when it comes to living in Christ, the conceptual leap is no leap at all. The Bible says that we find our lives by losing them. God is always giving away in order to find, and we are no exception.

Our doorway to recovery, to being cured of the chronic life, is to put the focus on others. After all, it is the need for self-focus and self-interest that causes the symptoms in the first place. Put the focus back on the Creator, and the Creation finds its answers again.

Many therapists and counselors will wholly disagree with the above strategy. But we believe that, although most of them are incredibly capable of helping in psychological and emotional concerns, the spiritually chronic life is diagnosed in relation to our connection or disconnection to what God has intended for us from the beginning. And thus, the CURE exists in how we rebuild that connection, not in how we teach each other to survive the separation.

SHANE: I recently preached a sermon series titled "Seven Degrees of Separation," based on the seven deadly sins. What I realized is that the seven deadly sins are meant not so much to harm us, which they do, but their real malady and harm are in how they damage our connection to God and to our brothers and sisters. The sin, whatever it may be, is symptomatic of a tool that, ultimately, is meant to harm all of us, not just one of us.

For instance, gluttony may seem that it is only affecting the body of the person in question. But *gluttony* is defined as "taking in more than we need." Thus, gluttony deprives others of those resources, and it affects the person in question so deeply that he or she is unable to participate in healthy community. So the person who actually is guilty of gluttony is just the first part of the real struggle, which also involves others.

Or what about lust? Is it just a means for corrupting a person's heart with the intimate temptations of wanting someone physically? Or, as Jesus says, is this a sin that redefines the heart? "As people thinketh, so are they" (Proverbs 23:7, paraphrased). Lust is not just about the person who lusts or even the person who is lusted after. It is about everyone that person will meet, and it is about the time the one who lusts will spend doing something other than being in relationship with God.

The chronic life, no matter how you qualify it, is a communal disease and illness. And the CURE must be communal in nature.

Friends, we hope you have seen this conceptual leap for yourselves over the time you have spent reading this book and through the forty days of the spiritual treatment plan. We realize this has not been easy. We have asked questions and required a process that likely has pushed you and challenged your stamina but also your heart. But we also hope you have seen that the leap is worth it. By getting out of your own way, hopefully you have found the real you and decided that you like what you see. We know God does.

And this is not the end of the story or the process. We encourage you to write down your thoughts or keep a journal, to keep praying, to keep studying your Bible, and to continue to put yourself in the shoes of others as you seek to understand their situations and the possibilities by the renewing of your mind. Keep striving to respond to the needs of others, because that is what the children of the Creator do, and then keep living as one another's advocates so that *no one*, no matter what the circumstance, will have to make this journey alone.

In 2007, a young man played a violin in one of the stations of the Washington D.C. Metro system. He played for forty-five minutes, including six selections from Bach. During his time playing, nearly two thousand people passed by, but only six stopped to listen or pay any attention at all. Four of the six were children, who were promptly dragged away by their parents to a waiting Metro train. The young man received just under thirty-two dollars from donations.

What people did not know was that this situation was an experiment set up by the *Washington Post*. The young man was Joshua Bell, one of the world's most celebrated and successful musicians. The violin he played had a value of $3.5 million. And just the night before, Mr. Bell had filled a Boston theater, where tickets sold for over $100 per seat.

The experiment concluded that beauty, outside of its context, is both underappreciated and undervalued. And the experiment also showed that if people missed such greatness and opportunity as one of the world's great musicians played for free in front of them, how much more are we missing in our daily routines? That is indeed a great question.

This story reminds us that beauty is all around us, and so is greatness. The God of the universe has been playing a song, *your* song, right in front of you for your entire life. Have you noticed? Or have we passed by, too busy to notice extravagance at our feet? (See Gene Weingarten, "Pearls Before Breakfast." *Washington Post*, April 8, 2007, http://www.washingtonpost.com/wp-dyn/content/article/2007/04/04/AR2007040401721.html [accessed July 25, 2010].)

God does not make promises that he does not intend to keep. If we are not enough on our own—and we know that we can't be—then he plans to fill in the gaps. If we are struggling, then he will provide the soothing guidance for a new direction. God's music is the finest. And it has been fashioned for us. We just have to notice and hear it. That is our prayer for you—a "new normal" and a new direction. This old, chronic life, this old concept, has had its run long enough. That time is over. Your time has come. Enjoy the journey. You have earned it. You deserve it because you are his. The music was written for you . . . yes, you. And that makes for a new beginning, exploding with awe and wonder, even if the context seems unchanged. Trust us. At times you won't believe what you hear and what you see, but you also won't doubt it either. It will sound oddly familiar. Because, remember, *this* melody is God's normal. *This* is what he has planned from the beginning; this is what, all along, he has had in store.

We love you.

DISCUSSION GUIDE

The Cure for the Chronic Life is built around a forty-day spiritual treatment plan that includes Scripture, personal reflections, and prayers for each day. If you are reading and discussing the book with a group, you will want to decide for yourselves the manner and pace by which you will cover the material. Reflection/discussion questions are provided for each of the seven chapters.

CHAPTER 1
THE SEVEN WORRIES OF LIVING IN CRISIS

1. What does it mean to be "living chronically in crisis" or "living a chronic life"? What are the results of living this way, and how does it affect a person's quality of life?

2. What chronic condition or conditions in your life do you feel you should identify and address? How do your struggles affect

your everyday activities, your day-to-day living, and also your relationships?

3. Reflect on / discuss the following statement: "Most chronic patterns do not start overnight."

4. How is "our normal" often different from "God's normal" or what God wants for our life?

5. List "The Seven Worries of Living in Crisis" outlined by the authors and briefly reflect on / discuss each one.

6. How do the seven worries keep us from living the life God wants for us? What role do our habits and patterns play?

7. Why is it often difficult to admit that "we are not enough"—that by ourselves, without God and without others, we don't have what it takes to live life in a way that is meaningful and fulfilling?

8. Acknowledging that we are not enough, the authors say, "But we also can't let these worries linger, and we can't let them continue pushing the point of our inadequacy back to us. That kind of life is death—death for our hopes, dreams, and relationships." Where do you think the balance is between knowing that "we alone are not enough" and finding the courage we need to confront our worries, deal with them, and overcome them?

9. Reflect on / discuss the following statement: "The human experience requires healthy relationships."

10. The authors say, "We have been built to crave life." What examples can you give showing this to be true?

11. What additional thoughts or ideas from this chapter would you like to explore?

CHAPTER 2
THE CURE

1. How do you typically deal with change? When is change good? What makes change sometimes difficult or scary?

2. In what ways has doubt held you back?

3. In what ways can change be considered a journey? Why is it important to have a conversation partner along for that journey?

4. What are the benefits of having a plan for dealing with challenges and making a change?

5. What does it mean to you personally to know that God doesn't want you to have to live "chronic in crisis," and that "God has something better in mind" for you? What does it take for you—or for anyone—to believe that?

6. What do the authors mean by the statement, "There is only so much we can discover by dwelling in the pain or in the confusion"? What is the importance of turning to the Bible when seeking direction for a better life?

7. What additional thoughts or ideas from this chapter would you like to explore?

CHAPTER 3
THE CURE: COMPASSION

1. In your own words, define *compassion*.

2. How did Jesus show compassion? What was his response to those who were hurting?

3. How important to compassion is the concept of making a "U-turn"? In what areas of your life do you need a "U-turn"? What keeps you from making those changes? What would making those changes look like in your life?

4. Read John 17:20-23, 26. How does it feel to know that Jesus is praying for you? How does Jesus' prayer for unity among you and your brothers and sisters challenge you to live your life differently?

5. What does it mean to be "of one mind" with Christ?

6. The authors write that "we often miss the needs of others because we are distracted by our own needs and our troubles." How can we open our eyes and our hearts to those who are hurting?

7. What are some of the "life chances" God provides for us, and how can we make the most of them? What does God expect from us in return for our receiving a "life chance"?

8. What does it mean to be a neighbor? In what ways do neighbors show compassion for one another?

9. Describe the value of friends, and of friendship. Read John 14:15-17. What does it mean to you to think of God as your friend?

10. What does it mean to build your life on a solid foundation? How can we strengthen the foundation of our life?

11. What does it mean that we are all part of the family of God? How does God wish for us to respond to the needs of others around us? What opportunities for showing compassion can you identify in your community right now, and what commitment can you make to doing so?

12. What additional thoughts or ideas from this chapter would you like to explore?

CHAPTER 4
THE CURE: UNDERSTANDING

1. In your own words, define *understanding*. How does the chronic life keep us "in the dark" and "out of the know"? What happens when we continually live this way?

2. What do you think the authors mean when they say, "The more we understand of God's world and God's children, the more we actually 'learn' about ourselves"? They also write that our relationships are "the picture we paint of our faith in action." In what ways have you seen this to be true?

3. Reflect on / discuss the following statement: "Worship is the way we understand God. And if we are to understand our world, it helps to spend time understanding the Creator first."

4. Read Matthew 6:5-13. What is the significance of Jesus showing the disciples how to pray by giving them the Lord's Prayer,

rather than *telling* them how to pray? According to the authors, why does the Lord's Prayer work better as an outline?

5. Reflect on / discuss the meaning of the phrase "spiritual emancipation." What does it mean to be free in Christ?

6. What do the authors mean by "a God Reality," and how does that differ from what the world offers? Read Luke 12:25-34; in this passage, where is Jesus telling us to put our trust?

7. What are some of the reasons we may overlook or ignore the needs of those around us? What role does basic human understanding play in recognizing and responding to others' needs?

8. What would you include in a healthy "spiritual diet"? What are some of the results of not following a healthy spiritual diet?

9. How does pride get in the way of our following Jesus' example? What do we learn from the Bible regarding forgiveness and second chances?

10. For Christians, what does it mean to live passionately? In what ways do you think God may be calling you to be a "game changer"?

11. Reflect on / discuss the following statement: "Wisdom and reason do not drop from the sky. They begin at home." Why is it important to connect to people of character and integrity? What persons of character and integrity can you turn to for guidance and help?

12. What additional thoughts or ideas from this chapter would you like to explore?

CHAPTER 5
THE CURE: RESPONSE

1. What does it mean to say that "all of us are called to *respond* to whatever God is doing in our lives"? What are some ways in which we can identify our spiritual gifts and determine the areas in which we feel God is calling us to respond?

2. The authors say, "When we get our hands into the muck of someone else's life and work at making a difference, we pull back the veil of our own situation, and real healing can begin." Reflect on / discuss this question: how do we know when to stop assessing our own situation and reach out to help someone else?

3. In what ways does Jesus push us out of our comfort zones? What does it mean to be "the hands and feet of Jesus"?

4. Jesus asked the man by the pool, "Do you want to get well?" Reflect on / discuss the balance between desiring to get well, having the courage to get well, taking practical steps to getting well, and praying and trusting in God. How do these fit together? What other components are there to moving out of the chronic life?

5. What keeps you from asking for God to heal the whole of your life? What does real healing mean for you? Make a list of what keeps you "by the pool" and from being healed. What do you need to "set down" in your life in order to respond to God's urging to be healed and begin again?

6. What does it mean to you personally to know that "no matter how much we love those who are most dear to us, God loves us even more"? What does it mean that "God's love is greater than anything we can know"?

7. The authors say, "When we hear the voice of God, we find our life." What does it sound like to you personally to hear the voice of God? What does God offer to us when we drop everything and follow God?

8. Read Acts 16:25-34, which tells the story of Paul and Silas. What example did Paul and Silas set while in captivity? Why do you think their jailer responded the way he did? Why is it so important to model God's grace for others, as Paul and Silas did?

9. In what significant ways are we connected to God's Creation? What responsibilities do we have in caring for Creation and in caring for our brothers and sisters?

10. Read Romans 8:31-39 and reflect on / discuss the following statement: "We must choose to reject the notion that all is 'what it will be.' God does not see it that way. Instead, he knows 'how it should be' and reshapes our paths."

11. The authors distinguish between "playing a game of faith" and "the real thing." What does *real faith* mean to you, and what does it require of us?

12. What additional thoughts or ideas from this chapter would you like to explore?

CHAPTER 6
THE CURE: ENCOURAGEMENT

1. Shane shares the story of his Sunday school teacher, Mrs. Gandy, who gave him much needed encouragement as a child.

Who has been an encourager or advocate for you in your life, and what has this person (or these persons) meant to you?

2. Reflect on / discuss the following statement: "Simply knowing Jesus is not enough. We must become Christ for our world." In what ways is encouragement a *privilege* to the one who provides it?

3. What are we to do when someone doesn't respond to our encouragement?

4. What does it mean to believe in someone? How does it feel to know that someone believes in you? Why do healthy covenant friendships make such a difference in our lives and in our faith?

5. Make a list of your love- and grace-generators, those special people in your life with whom you share a mutually supportive bond of encouragement and love. Which persons on your list need a word of encouragement from you today? How can you make the encouragement of friends and family a consistent part of your spiritual practices?

6. What do the authors mean when they say God's goal is to "make the heavy life light"? What do you think is God's role in the midst of our struggles and disappointments? Why is it often hard to let go of disappointments?

7. The authors tell us, "As Christians, we have a special duty not to jump to conclusions." What example does Christ set for us in this regard?

8. What is meant by the statement, "We don't get to choose with whom and when we share God's love"?

9. Jesus tells us that "with God all things are possible" (see Matthew 19:26; Mark 9:23). What does that mean for you? How are we to deal with what may seem to be unanswered requests? What part do we play in helping others face their doubt and drawing closer to Christ?

10. Deanna shares the story of the bookmark that includes the words "Love means . . ."; what does love mean to you? What are the by-products of love?

11. Read 2 Corinthians 5:14-21. How do these words speak to you, and what do they say about a new beginning and new life? How does it feel knowing that God wants to draw you close and heal your hurts? How do we achieve our potential by "giving ourselves away"?

12. What additional thoughts or ideas from this chapter would you like to explore?

CHAPTER 7
THE SEVEN WONDERS OF LIVING IN CHRIST

1. What does it mean to live "chronic in Christ"? How does living in Christ enable us to deal with our worries?

2. List "The Seven Wonders of Living in Christ" outlined by the authors, and briefly reflect on / discuss each one.

3. Reflect on / discuss the following statement: "Real, healthy relationships are not meant to be complex or complicated . . . they are simple and lived out in love, grace, forgiveness, and

purpose." What are your thoughts on the idea that "when one person is in control, a relationship cannot survive very long"?

4. The authors say, "God has made us family, not simply acquaintances, and certainly not strangers." What does this mean for us as Christians, and how should it affect our daily lives?

5. How does the chronic life make us feel as though we have to "go it alone"? In what ways does God let us know that this isn't the case?

6. Reflect on / discuss the following statement: "A life lived in Christ craves meaning—real meaning that is not a facsimile of us but takes on the very image of Christ in us."

7. What does it take to move from a "just-getting-by" mentality to living with a sense of purpose? What are the benefits of living with a sense of purpose?

8. What does it mean to live with compassion and conviction?

9. How does the chronic life tear away at our relationships and loyal commitments? How does living in Christ bring restoration? What does it mean to you to know that Jesus' commitment to you lasts forever?

10. What does it mean to manage your energies wisely? Give some examples from your own life of how you accomplish this or how you might better accomplish it.

11. How can we steer ourselves away from self-centeredness or a "quid pro quo mind-set" and toward genuine selflessness? What does it mean to put God in control of our lives?

12. In what ways is the cure for the chronic life "communal" in nature? How will you remind yourself on your journey that you are surrounded by the love of God in Christ, that countless others are walking with you, and that you are not alone?

13. What additional thoughts or ideas from this chapter would you like to explore?

14. What new perspectives or insights do you have as a result of your reading, reflection, and discussion of this book? What tools or resources do you feel you have now that you didn't have or weren't aware of before? What challenges remain for you, and how will you meet those challenges? What new possibilities do you see ahead?